W9-BMW-684

# Praise for *Courage*

"*Courage* offers insightful advice for executives who wish to do *good*, while doing *well*, showing them how ethics and character can lead to increased profits and loyal customers. But the most important audience for this book may be the rising generation of business leaders, particularly MBA students. *Courage* offers them an important perspective that's often absent from their course work."

> —Donald L. McCabe, professor of management and global business, Rutgers Business School, and founding president of the Center for Academic Integrity, Duke University

"I look at this wonderful book through my combat experiences in Vietnam and thirty years in the FBI. Gus Lee has hit the nail on the head. He's captured the essence of leadership. Want to be a true leader? It's in *Courage*."

> —Charles Hickey, FBI Special Agent (retired)

"Gus Lee fans who enjoy curling up with the trademark eloquence of his storytelling will not be disappointed by *Courage*. His demand for leading with courage comes not from a suspender-snapping CEO; it comes from a humble immigrant and former soldier whose astonishing achievements were built on guts and integrity. Lee argues for courage with the strong voice of humility. It is his voice—a voice of uncommon power that will embolden every reader."

> —Bill Robinson, president, Whitworth College

"As the Old Sarge once said, 'All I want from my officers is bravery. Brave is enough.' Gus Lee is a full-tilt practitioner of the principles in this book. His life has been filled with moments of grave challenge, and those who know and have served with him, both in and out of the Army, know he writes of courage from first-hand experience. That is why he can tell just the right story that links Confucius and Aristotle to the gut-wrenchers of daily modern life, and make it ring strong and true."

—James P. Sullivan Jr., president of Sullivan Technology, Inc.; teacher of creativity and problem solving, Purdue University; former infantry officer and Army aviator

"Gus Lee and I worked together in a start-up technology company for two years. Gus was one of the cofounders. Weak leadership threatened the company's viability and necessitated bold action to preclude failure. Gus had the courage to lead the way for major change and thereby save the enterprise. Gus lives what he teaches. Integrity, courage, and character are action words to him, not just theoretical concepts. *Courage* is a leadership book that demands to be added to your professional library—but only if you are determined to be successful."

—James R. Ellis, Lieutenant General, U.S. Army (retired); cofounder of three technology companies; CEO of a children's charity in Florida

"Gus Lee has identified *the critical element* that determines outcomes for executives and for organizations. I've studied, written about, and coached courageous leaders for nearly two decades; this book captures the learnable behaviors they have in common. I look forward to sharing Lee's clear insights with my clients in business, in government, in academia, and the nonprofit world—with anyone who would be a better leader."

—Ed Ruggero, leadership and ethics guide, and coauthor of the U.S. Army Field Manual *Army Leadership* and *The Leader's Compass*

"Many great books have been written on leadership, but Gus Lee strikes at the heart of the matter in *Courage*. He reminds us what we know to be true, but don't want to face and see rejected in everyday life. Most important, he provides us the opportunity to reflect, while we read the stories he tells, on how we might change and become the leaders we know we can be."

—Pat Scully, president and CEO, Kids at Hope,
and former EDS Iran Rescue Mission member

"Gus Lee and Diane Elliott-Lee have raised the leadership issues relating to integrity, courage, and character to an entirely new level. This book is a must-read for anyone who aspires to be a leader of character."

—Len Marella, president, Center for Leadership and Ethics

"I was up before dawn reading this book. I find it an excellent read. It made me reflect on issues we deal with over the years which require us to be courageous; I think we have all stood at the edge looking at the river of fear. Gus Lee's use of stories is powerful."

—General Maureen LaBoeuf (retired),
first female head of department at West Point

"In *Courage*, Gus Lee brings a new perspective to the essence of great leadership. 'Courageous leadership' is an especially practical and powerful tool for the many expressions of leadership. Emerging leaders in politics, business, community, education and faith need to absorb the message Lee conveys."

—Bambang Budijanto, area director for Asia,
Compassion International

# Gus Lee
## with
## Diane Elliott-Lee

# Courage

## The Backbone of Leadership

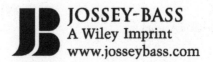

JOSSEY-BASS
A Wiley Imprint
www.josseybass.com

Copyright © 2006 by Gus Lee.

Published by Jossey-Bass
A Wiley Imprint
989 Market Street, San Francisco, CA 94103-1741    www.josseybass.com

No part of this publication may be reproduced, stored in a retrieval system, or transmitted in any
form or by any means, electronic, mechanical, photocopying, recording, scanning, or otherwise,
except as permitted under Section 107 or 108 of the 1976 United States Copyright Act, without
either the prior written permission of the publisher, or authorization through payment of the
appropriate per-copy fee to the Copyright Clearance Center, Inc., 222 Rosewood Drive,
Danvers, MA 01923, 978-750-8400, fax 978-646-8600, or on the Web at www.copyright.com.
Requests to the publisher for permission should be addressed to the Permissions Department,
John Wiley & Sons, Inc., 111 River Street, Hoboken, NJ 07030, 201-748-6011, fax 201-748-
6008, or online at www.wiley.com/go/permissions.

Limit of Liability/Disclaimer of Warranty: While the publisher and author have used their best
efforts in preparing this book, they make no representations or warranties with respect to the
accuracy or completeness of the contents of this book and specifically disclaim any implied
warranties of merchantability or fitness for a particular purpose. No warranty may be created or
extended by sales representatives or written sales materials. The advice and strategies contained
herein may not be suitable for your situation. You should consult with a professional where
appropriate. Neither the publisher nor author shall be liable for any loss of profit or any other
commercial damages, including but not limited to special, incidental, consequential, or other
damages.

Readers should be aware that Internet Web sites offered as citations and/or sources for further
information may have changed or disappeared between the time this was written and when it is
read.

Jossey-Bass books and products are available through most bookstores. To contact Jossey-Bass
directly call our Customer Care Department within the U.S. at 800-956-7739, outside the U.S.
at 317-572-3986, or fax 317-572-4002.

Jossey-Bass also publishes its books in a variety of electronic formats. Some content that appears
in print may not be available in electronic books.

**Library of Congress Cataloging-in-Publication Data**
Lee, Gus.
   Courage: the backbone of leadership/Gus Lee with Diane Elliott-Lee.
        p. cm.
   Includes bibliographical references and index.
   ISBN-13: 978-0-7879-8137-2 (cloth)
   ISBN-10: 0-7879-8137-0 (cloth)
   1. Leadership.  2. Courage.  3 Management.  I. Elliott-Lee, Diane.  II. Title.
   HD57.7.L4387    2006
   658.4'092—dc22

                                                        2006000529

Printed in the United States of America
FIRST EDITION
V10004928_100118

*To the marriage of*
*Ancient Wisdom*
*and*
*Modern Organizational Practices*

# Contents

# Courage

# INTRODUCTION

> Courage is rightly esteemed the first of human
> qualities . . . because it is the quality which
> guarantees all others.
>
> —*Winston Churchill*

I've worked with hundreds of bright and well-educated leaders in fifty industries and on every continent. Most are good people who are honorable in their private lives. But when they face the great river that cuts across all organizations, they remain on the safe near bank. On this bank, most business is done with reason and general fairness.

On the far bank live our crises, bad hires, weak ethics, questionable acts, misreporting, anger, jealousy, regrets and character-challenged managers. This is the stuff that demands dynamic and courageous leadership. Facing us is the River of Fear, made deep and wide by our hesitations, timidity, doubts, and paralysis.

How many fine and experienced execs boldly cross the river to challenge wrong behaviors and take risks for principles and for others? Not many. This is a crossable boundary, but most of us won't try it.

What do we know about the few who courageously do? They demand excellent conduct of others because they first require it of themselves. Their courage inspires prodigious results. This allows these classic leaders to find work-and-life balance, to love their families and to enjoy private lives. They tend to be happier and more content.[1]

## We Are Built to Cross Rivers

That's why Churchill, as Great Britain faced a grand moral and national crisis, deemed courage "the first of all human qualities." Aristotle said that courageous virtue is the essence of not just happiness but life itself.

Cowardice is the great opposite. Instead of building, it ruins. Fear begins in our guts and spreads into families and organizations. Living in fear is not living; it is tantamount to being a prisoner of our own weaknesses, constantly awaiting the next injustice.

Thus courage—or its absence—determines all outcomes. Modestly put, courage decides quality of life and personal as well as institutional success.

Courage is so crucial that it sits in the heart of us. That's why we can't help but admire and follow courage until we demonstrate it.

Courage—not brashness, greed, or recklessness—was, early in our evolution, the *one quality* needed for human survival. It brilliantly linked learning, communication, and teamwork to social advantage. Using courage, we slow, daylight-limited bipeds without fangs, claws, wings, armor, or four legs could subordinate our egos for the good of the clan. We could defeat the fast, lethal, night-visioned predator quadrupeds that still inhabit our collective memory—that make little kids peer under their beds at night and cause them to awaken with sudden, branch-grabbing spasms.

Long before the invention of the corporation, we were hardwired to show courage regardless of risk to ourselves. Here's what is interesting: even today, without courage, nothing—from our relationships to our firms—is safe.

Heroism's era has not passed. It is here, before us, for in truth, no generation, regardless of war, peace, depression, or prosperity, is spared the need to demonstrate courage.

No individual, organization, or society comes to character without struggle. We should welcome moral struggles but have told our children that if they win in academics, they'll succeed in life. This runs counter to everything that wisdom teaches, and the results of this falsehood are becoming obvious.

There is much we do not control. Yet we have a tailor-made opportunity to build our individual and collective courage.

## Courage and You

I want to equip you to cross the river, for three things are certain. First, you and your organizations will face Points of Decision. Second, the power of courageous behaviors are well known. Third, you will need courage to cross.

I've seen the water many times and been required to face my many swarming fears. After early and later failures—many of them the stuff of novels—I learned to accept the challenge.

If an asthmatic, legally blind, babble-mouthed kid from a Chinese immigrant family who struggled on the streets of an inner-city black ghetto and in the engineering halls of West Point could do it, you certainly can, with far more grace and far less difficulty.

When we master the skills that are the competence of courage, we confidently enact bold leadership practices, translating the first human quality (courage) into effective and inspiring actions of true excellence.

I have watched executives and managers replace behaviors of timidity, doubt, and hesitation with the high conduct of courage. With each iteration, they grew their courage competence. With each act, they inspired those around them to their best selves. Over time, they built enduring teams and deep leadership benches. They reinstalled a sense of worth and camaraderie into their work environments.

They began, like all of us, as good people. They didn't cheat. But they wouldn't repair conflicts. They didn't lie, but they tolerated gossip and avoided dialogue with bullies who hurt coworkers and impaired the efforts of employees. Under pressure, these good people refused to cross the river of their own fears to do the right thing for others. They silently chose inaction and tolerated the unheroic long-term destructive consequences of fear.

What my clients discovered was that courage was not something with which we are born. That tall, physically powerful, and imposing males have no special aptitude for courage, for each of us has fair and equal access to the first human quality.

Clients discovered that courage—facing fear, acting for what is right, correcting wrongs in oneself, and addressing problems—could be developed and strengthened through practice. Courage is a learned quality, an acquirable set of skills, a practiced competence. It's like boxing, except it's easier, it smells better, and it causes fewer nosebleeds.

We have seen this truth since earliest human times. Moses, Joshua, Confucius, Aristotle, Abraham Lincoln, Eleanor Roosevelt, Winston Churchill, Mahatma Gandhi, Albert Einstein, and Harper Lee teach us through their lives and writing about both the accessibility and the centrality of courage in human affairs.

## Points of Decision

They, like us, faced Points of Decision. Points of Decision are key institutional intersections where crises test our high core values.

Whirlpool entered a Point of Decision (POD) when it failed to meet revenue goals. MCI faced a POD when it considered merging its fiber-optic transmission network with WorldCom's backbone services. Kimberly-Clark faced a POD when it considered selling its mills. You'll read about these examples, and many more, at various places in this book.

Character-based institutions prepare for PODs by bulking up on courage. In PODs, key executives are predictably pressured and are expected to respond with character. Research proves that only in this singular way do we realize sustainable and outstanding results.

But even though we clearly need principled people in times of crisis, few organizations courageously prepare for their inevitable PODs.

What stops us? We resist repairing bad habits. We also resist change.

Yet principled conduct under pressure is a simple concept. It has two working parts: (1) establishment of high core values and (2) courageous behaviors in alignment with those core values.

When firms fail, it doesn't take Sherlock Holmes and a galloping herd of bloodhounds to find the trail. Through the smoke and flames, we can still see the Point of Decision, where crisis tested values and firms were found lacking in the practice of principled conduct.

We need courage and character at our PODs.

## The Lost Path

A survey of today's busy business shelves reveals no book that explains how to have courage—or how to develop it personally or grow it organizationally. Human courage, the primary competence that saw us through Paleolithic species-threatening hazards and led the United States against the greatest empires in history, is no longer in our national consciousness.

We didn't mean to stop developing character. No one would consciously choose to make expensive daily personal sacrifices of hard-earned well-being on the altar of fear. But while chasing increasingly elusive success, we lost our way.

In our families, universities, schools, communities, and institutions, we accidentally canceled our central national life quality program—character development. In that dimmed light, we have treated the observations of Moses, Aristotle, and Confucius as academic trivia questions instead of as demonstrated truths defining the quality of life. We actually began to believe that we no longer needed wisdom.

Courage is universal. It is needed by each of us in every conceivable circumstance. Courage, to our benefit, is a constant. I learned this as a boy fighting to be accepted as an American on the streets of San Francisco, as a deputy district attorney convicting criminals, as a senior executive with offices in three cities, as a vice-president advocating high core values, as an executive coach, as a corporate and government consultant in many fields, and as a husband and father.

I want you to have the essential gift of courage. We should all experience the benefits of courageous habits not only for ourselves but also for the people and organizations with whom we share our lives.

## Coaching for Courage

I once asked Coach Tony for one punch that I could use to win every fight. "Best punch is yur left hook," he said. I nodded eagerly. "Hook inta the bag about twenty thousand times. Then it'll be yur best punch."

He had taught me this when I understood nothing. After I had followed his advice to the point of exhaustion, he showed me more. *Plant left foot forward, chin in, right glove up. Cock left arm, aim for the head, breathe. Swing with a grunt through the bag from the hip, pivoting on the left, a door on a jewel.*

*Make it whistle. Recover! Again! Again! Again! Snap lead left jab! Three hooks—Joe Louis could put five together— now right hook, snap, jab, jab! Left hook—again! Again! Right lead, snap jab, left hook, right hook, three left hooks! Didja feel that? All right! Do it again.*

Because I was coached, I can coach you. You won't have to bob and weave, get arm-weary, get a busted nose, or need a transfusion. But through the pages of this book, we will develop the reproducible behaviors of courage.

## True Stories

*Courage: The Backbone of Leadership* uses true stories from Whirlpool, Kaiser Permanente, IntegWare, and other actual organizations. This lets us observe executives as they face and overcome the worries and fears that confront us all. For you will also be required to face your own private and institutional Points of Decision. Everyone does.

We'll watch these executives use the behaviors of courage to produce extraordinary and reproducible results. We'll also watch their very smart, gifted, experienced, and worry-burdened counterparts fail.

Their collective examples offer us practical lessons, practice opportunities, and operational to-do's that we can apply to our decisions on leadership's playing fields.

We can use the transformational power of courage to lead effective change.

After reading this book, you will own the tools to transform yourself, your organization, and your family.

## Organization of the Book

This book is a primer on courage. It has three parts.

In Part One, we watch Chris Kay of IntegWare approach several Points of Decision. We learn what happens when courage is not considered and what happens when it is.

Through Chris's story, we will experience the call to courage, the obstacles in our path, and the emancipation from fear and failure when values-based, principled, courageous behaviors are employed.

We will see ourselves in Chris's story.

Part Two, "Courage in Action," is the book's core.

Courage is manifested in courageous communication, courageous leadership, courageous problem-solving, and in resolving high-end conflicts.

These tools and skills constitute the competence of courage and are presented in a progression of learning based on programs that have been presented to Levi Strauss, Kaiser Permanente, Whirlpool, ISEC, IntegWare, West Point, the FBI, the U.S. Department of Justice, the Young Presidents Organization, Centura Hospitals, the Smithsonian Institution, the La Jolla Conference, various colleges and universities, the National Conference of Supreme Court Justices, and since 1994, West Point's National Conference on Ethics in America.

We first learn the three base skills: courageous communication, courageous leadership, and courageous problem solving. We're then ready to enter corporate tiger country to learn to face and fix high-end conflicts and mend gut-wrenching personal, departmental, and institutional feuds.

Part Three, "Growing Your Courage," concludes with a set of take-away practices. These equip you to fight entropy—the natural erosion and retrogression of values, integrity, and skills.

Throughout the book, we learn to use specific tools and measurements to apply the behaviors of courage in everyday situations.

Life is demanding. Luckily, there is one quality that drives transformational leadership and personal and institutional success.

That one quality is courage, Churchill's prime human quality.

One day, I passed the final test to become a YMCA junior leader. Coach Tony gave me a key to the Central Y; I could open up the gym for other kids, turn on the lights, line up the gear against the walls, and start training classes with warm-ups and answering questions.

With this book, you can open up doors for your organization, for your family, and for your life.

You can turn on the lights for yourself and others.

You can make uncommon courage common.

# Part One

# BACKBONE AT THE POINT OF DECISION

Here's a truth: principled leaders solve moral problems. They have the courage to act rightly. They consistently demonstrate principled conduct under pressure.

This gives them the strong spine to be effective and envied leaders. Backbone is what everyone admires, everyone needs, everyone wants, and everyone follows.

Courage is the single most decisive trait in a leader. This is because personal and organizational crises are as routine and predictable as midtown cabs and sirens, and a manager without courage is as useful as a rowboat in a bullfight.

Leaders with courage lend backbone to their organizations. Then, when institutions face their Points of Decision—when serious crises test actual core values and therefore an institution's future—both leaders and institutions can act rightly and powerfully.

In Part One, we'll meet actual executives in real firms who strive to apply courage and high core values to the types of problems and challenges we all face. We'll watch as they develop courage and backbone in themselves, their companies, and their families.

# 1

# CHRIS'S STORY

Courage is not simply one of the virtues but the
form of every virtue at the testing point.

—C. S. *Lewis*

IntegWare is a product life cycle management software company
that serves Accenture, Agilent, Apple, General Electric, General
Motors, Hewlett-Packard, Johnson & Johnson, NEC, Siemens,
TRW, and many other Fortune 1000 firms.

IntegWare's CEO is Christopher Armstrong Kay, a square-
shouldered, clean-cut, tightly organized Hewlett-Packard engineering veteran who took IntegWare's helm when it was trying to
choose between breaking into pieces and diving off a cliff.

Like most executives, he didn't think that courage would be at
the center of his recovery operation. He was focused on staff, deliverables, productivity, brains, quality, speed, and revenues.

Like most execs, Chris didn't relish crisis. A glance at his organized desk and the neat press of his clothing suggests that he prefers
a well-disciplined shop to one with trash fires, cracking floors, and
nervous customers. Chris was acutely conscious of high operating
principles when he took the helm. This put him ahead in a tough
game, but this is one of those deep advantages that is not immediately visible.

Chris had arrived long after IntegWare had sped past its first
major crises and Points of Decision—those key moments when crisis tests principles. Years earlier, key IntegWare managers should
have been replaced by leaders with character. Years earlier, ethical

relationships should have been preserved against the pressures of expediency, denial, puffery, self-interest, and favoritism.

Weeks after he had positioned his family pictures in his new office, the historical bills for low and poorly performed core values came due. The firm was no longer beguiled by a choice of a stark either-or; it was now actively breaking up *and* sliding down a cliff.

In its free fall down Darwin's ladder, IntegWare had lost its moorings. Its people wrestled for survival using prehistoric tools: backstabbing, gossip, rumors, and panic followed by the departure of some and the fears of all. This is super material for a teen horror film but unwelcome conditions for a good company.

Infighting had split the firm; debt capacity was at redline; printers spat out résumés; customers were worried; and work had become as much fun as exchanging gunfire in evening traffic. Yet it somehow continued to deliver products. IntegWare needed cash, customers, talent, strategic planning, core values, leadership, teamwork, a retreat, and new coffeemakers. *But in what order?*

Order is elusive when hearts and minds are lost in the fogs of economic struggle, fearful choices, and family despair.

Chris, like Aristotle, could separate the essential from the important, the necessary from the pressing. The Greeks called this ability *diaphoranta*. It enables great decision making.

In the winds of unit disorder and private miseries, Chris saw the essential fact about his firm: *We have no operating principles around which to mount a recovery, no core values serving as the unifying behavioral standard for the firm's next level of performance.* He saw that everything other than values was secondary.

Chief Operating Officer Will Sampson, a big, steady Iowan, would help. Sampson agreed to run the shop, maintain quality, and manage internal customer relations. Most important, he would work with the staff to develop new company core values while Chris sprinted around the globe reassuring customers and meeting with employees, asking them to stay and trust him.

Chris quickly set sample core values (*integrity, teamwork, innovation, customer focus*, borrowed from an earlier firm) for company consideration, wrote code in emergencies, brought in meals for late-night workers, picked up trash to suggest good order, got new contracts for down-range revenues, gave up sleep for Lent, and quashed vicious company rumors for fun. Attrition stopped. His efforts were allowing a glimpse of sunlight.

It was then that a history of IntegWare delays and unresolved internal and external conflicts caught up with the company. These issues had been hounding the company and now they arrived, panting, tired, angry, and demanding. They cost cash, damaged relationships, and reduced supplementary support needed for key deliverables. Soured relationships turned bitter. Blaming became viral. Sullen silence settled like a Grand Banks fog. People began leaving again. You could feel it: the ship was sinking. Emergency funds were urgently needed, and strategy was out. The company was down to finding immediate tactical responses for the hour and the moment.

Chris met with Will Sampson, who had failed to begin the core values process or solve a single office conflict. But Sampson agreed to carry 35 percent of the debt to refloat a crucial line of credit. Chris would shoulder the rest. But Will missed the key bank appointment, apologized, and then missed the rescheduled meetings.

Standing alone in a sunny parking lot after another canceled bank meeting, Chris grimaced, as if small muscular flexions could dispel all bad feeling. To the casual observer, Chris appeared intact, but his insides were flopping on the concrete.

He thought: *Look at the facts. You're on notice that Will is a major problem.* For a moment, Chris wasn't standing in the Rockies. He was back being a second-grader in his Dallas home. His parents had quietly closed the kitchen door to say whatever sad things they said to each other when they tried, without success, to fix their problems. He and Ellen, his five-year-old sister, tried to listen through the thick door, hoping to hear good things but needing even more to deny the truth.

The truth was that their parents couldn't resolve their differences. They were good people, but they lacked the skills. For years, they had unintentionally been installing the vast childhood fears of separation and abandonment deep into the psyches of their small children. The parents resorted, as many of us do, to trying to cover up reality for others instead of learning new skills for themselves.

Chris's father left the home that year, never to return. Chris's dad remained active in the Boy Scouts and camping. A few times, he took Chris fishing at big, blue Lake Texarkana. There the father and son sat silently and uncomfortably, studying their bobbers, praying for the nibble that would let them feel something together and magically recover the father's lost commitment.

Chris shook his head. He had to confront Will Sampson and figure out why his COO was a no-do and a no-show. *Why would a man say he'd do something and not do it? What do I do about this now? We're in a punctured lifeboat fighting for our lives.*

Chris returned to the office to plug holes. He realized that he couldn't afford the possibility that Will Sampson wasn't going to come through. IntegWare couldn't survive the year without a bailout, and that required Will. Chris set another appointment with him. In the next weeks, he kept accepting Will's increasingly weak excuses for not delivering the goods in core values development, results, and cash.

Chris was worried about Dornier Klein, a major Fortune 500 client whose overseas financial firms IntegWare had served for years. Chris's predecessor had warned him about this company.

"Dornier Klein doesn't like us. They only love Gene Stingley."

Gene Stingley was one of IntegWare's most brilliant thinkers and its most relationally challenged manager. He had performed intellectual wonders for Klein and had an unusually tight relationship with Klein's CIO, CTO, and COO. Klein had included Gene in every major in-house corporate event and party in Europe, Asia, and North America.

Then Chris received a call from Klein's CEO. Chris greeted him.

The Klein CEO bluntly told Chris that he should name Gene Stingley COO of IntegWare. "If you don't, I'm going to hire Stingley away from you. Chris, I'd save a lot of money having him in my own shop. My guess is that naming him COO is easier than all the alternatives."

Chris politely said he'd think about the idea and get back to the man. Quickly calling HR, Chris was told that Gene Stingley had refused to update his noncompete clause for over a decade. Thus Gene was probably free to work for Klein or for anyone else.

Chris checked the time, which was running unnaturally fast. He thought of speaking directly to Gene Stingley, remembering how difficult it was to even mention his special relationship with Klein.

A project engineer came to a scheduled appointment to explain that a major product data management proposal had been critically underbid by a sales exec.

"This isn't the first time this has happened," she said. It needed immediate modification before key consultants became unavailable. Chris was asking her cost questions when an essential contracting administrator, on the edge of tears, opened the door, stood awkwardly, and blurted out that he needed a month off, immediately.

"I'll be right with you," said Chris. "Be in your office in ten."

Chris's investment banker called, saying it was urgent. Chris asked the engineer to begin the modification orders and made a note to talk to the VP of sales. He picked up the phone to learn that the call truly was urgent; he now had major treasury and investment issues.

His assistant placed the two late and troubled operations summaries—needing his immediate quality and cost review—on his desk, next to his uneaten lunch and untouched breakfast burrito.

He scanned his e-mail. One of his department heads had written an urgent note: *You need to know that I can't work with Sly Travers anymore.* Travers was a senior manager.

He had a flashback to a Marx Brothers movie with a stateroom and fifty waiters, butlers, maids, and shoeshine men trying to work while jammed together like fruit in a blender. Will Sampson opened the door in a rare appearance. He motioned for Chris to get off the phone. Behind Will, Chris saw Gene Stingley whispering to a testing manager who was one of Will Sampson's main office allies.

Chris looked at the clock: time for Heather's soccer game. One minute to catch up with the administrator. He wondered what Will Sampson would say. He needed to make it home for dinner once this week. Well, maybe next quarter. Suddenly, he remembered that his son Grant had written him a note. He fished it from his pocket:

*Daddy, I want to rassle with you tonight. Love, Grant.*

*I wish,* he thought. Grant was a bright lad who watched his father's eyes and every movement as if they held the answers to the cosmos. Last night, Chris had returned home late, again. He had run up to Grant's bedroom. In the dark, he sensed that his son was feigning sleep, like a lost bear cub trying to trick a Texarkana mountain lion. Chris wanted to say something. His mouth opened, but no words came.

The meetings with the contracting administrator and Sampson were not wonderful. He had to allow the administrator to take time off and realized that he would have to somehow secure total firm refinancing by himself.

Chris looked at his watch; he had to send a memo to the board. The chairman was concerned about the status of new RFP responses. He outlined the board memo and picked up his private line.

Suppressing a mild inclination toward panic, Chris called a consultant for advice.

The consultant asked him to name the *diaphoranta*—the essential issue facing him.

"My COO, Will Sampson. International IBM experience. Top schools. Very, very smart. Great presence. And he's killing me."

The consultant asked Chris to describe Will's character, Will's ability to consistently sustain integrity-based behaviors.

"I guess not good," said Chris. "He's lying. I don't know why."

"How does that answer inform your next step?"

Pause. "I guess I have to ask him to step down."

The consultant remained silent.

"You saying I should fire him?" asked Chris.

The consultant took a moment. "If Will were on the market today, would you hire him?"

"No way."

"I think that's your answer."

"But he's a good man. He's just in a bad place right now. A lot of people trust him, and he has family problems. It's not serious or long-term, but I can't fire him."

The consultant was sympathetic. "Family issues make it tougher emotionally. Do you have any options to help him if he left?"

"I think I'd rather carry him than fire him."

The consultant got the details: Will Sampson had not performed crucial core tasks and had lied about his commitments. Staff knew of his failures to deliver. There were no indications he'd improve despite Chris's many attempts to counsel him on performance.

The consultant suggested that Chris get a thorough background check on his COO and then identify the right thing to do.

Chris learned that Will had a history of poor execution at IntegWare. Friends at IBM shared confidentially that Will was popular, but for unclear reasons, he had left under a cloud.

Chris grimaced. He had erred by interpreting the suggestion of competence for the presence of integrity. That error was now inflicting moral and economic risks on the company and himself.

He asked his assistant to hold his calls. He needed to discern.

Chris imagined firing Will. Instantly, he felt a jolt of fear: at least two mission-essential managers were Will's allies; Will could take them with him. Will, like Gene Stingley, also had a special relationship with another key customer who was on the bubble with IntegWare.

He also knew that he couldn't name Gene Stingley his COO— the man had always been a lone ranger, the brilliant mind at his desk. As a result, he lacked the kind of relational capital inside the company that a COO requires. Chris pictured telling Klein's CEO that he couldn't do what the CEO asked and then watching Gene and millions in revenues walk out the door.

Despite the fact that life didn't feel good right now, Chris Kay knew that he had at least ten good reasons to not fire Will and five reasons to not get into a pushing contest with Dornier Klein over the brilliant Gene Stingley.

Chris disliked conflict and hated the bad feelings in his gut that conflicts generate. But conflicts were impeding the work of his company. It was time to do what was essential.

Chris reflected on his immediate goals. *I need cash, an unsecured line of credit, and a new COO. Have to fix customer relationships and use teamwork to name core values. Use them to unify fragmented departments and cliques. Get home this year to see my family. I want to date my wife Janet and generate a new sales strategic plan as part of a new overall strategy. Keep up quality, develop board relationships. I have to rassle Grant and read to Heather. Get new sales execs. Cut senior exec salaries and stop mine altogether, today. And improve the coffee.*

He called HR to stop his own salary. But most important, Chris Kay had to identify his core personal values before his company could find its own.

# 2

# SEEKING COURAGEOUS
# CORE VALUES

We must become the change we want to see in the world.

—*Mahatma Gandhi*

I was the leadership consultant that Chris Kay had called.

Learning about IntegWare's challenges and seeing the clear need for courage, I couldn't help but remember my own early weaknesses and doubts about my own resolve.

Anne Lamott wrote in *Operating Instructions* that she delayed having children because she knew that someday her son would have to face the medieval horrors of junior high school.[1]

Given the choice as a lad, I would've bypassed life altogether. I felt uncomfortable in my own skin because I didn't like it and wasn't particularly fond of anyone else's. Not only did I wish I were a different person, but I wanted to be in a different world, such as Pluto.

I am proof that the time of miracles has never left us, for I was so scared about so many things that my goose bumps had their own planetary systems. Even the most challenged of us can achieve the behaviors of courage. I know this because I have been able to see this competence even though I arrived unable to even spell it.

"C'mere, kid," said Coach Tony, putting his conduitlike arm around my shoulders and pulling me into his office.

"You got the shirt; you're a Junior Leader with a whistle. Means you're supposed to watch over the Beginners. See them bigger kids? They're bruisin' the squirts and poundin' the shrimps. That's wrong.

You don't see it, and *that's* wrong. Probably cuz that's how you wuz treated."

I often felt stupid the moment Coach began to guide me. *Dumb China Boy always do wrong thing*, I told myself. *This too hard.*

But his look and his patience tipped my doubts and quelled my fears. Today, I wonder if he knew the impact of his installing in me the wild idea that I could learn and improve and become a man.

His look said, *See what I see, then do what I do.* His patience meant, *I'll lead you. I got time to teach you right.*

"When you correct them bullies, go gentle," he added, seeing my impetuosity to act. "Remember how I treated you."

For years, I thought Tony was teaching me how to fight. In a way, I was both wrong and right. He was teaching me to behave according to values and rules instead of in response to fear or need.

Tony was teaching me to care about others. Maybe he got it from his father, had it confirmed in the streets of Brooklyn, and had it wired in by the Marine Corps. I saw that my apathy about values grew out of apathy about people. When I was unprincipled with others, I was without high core values inside myself.

Have you ever seen a photo of Aristotle's bust? It's a strong, square face with high cheekbones, full beard, straight nose, and pronounced brows. Tony had the same-shaped head with a heavy five o'clock shadow at nine A.M. and a nose and ears that had said hello too many times to old American leather. But Tony and Aristotle knew *diaphoranta*: what is essential.

Tony was guiding me toward values-centered living—toward being an adult who, regardless of my lack of certainty and the yodeling of my fears, would cross the river and stand for principle and for others.

## Seduced by Avoidance

As Chris shared the organization's difficulties, I was reminded that his issues are universal; we all face them. They play out in every organization and family we know. They even exist in elite institutions that specialize in courageous communication and disciplined teamwork. For no matter who we are and what we do, we are seduced by avoidance.

Smart, well-educated cream-of-the-crop lawyers, M.B.A.'s, and business analysts at firms for which I never worked—Enron, Arthur Andersen, Warner-Lambert, Lexus, Adelphia, Addressograph, and a hundred other top corporations—saw wrongful acts, looked away, denied what they saw, covered up, left for different jobs, or simply ground down their molars.

After MCI became WorldCom, highly ethical senior executives with whom I worked did not challenge WorldCom's Bernie Ebbers and his radical 90-degree turn from strict MCI accounting and operating principles. These incredibly smart and gifted people hoped that vast profits would cure the risks against principles and best business practices.

I was once on a board with Ph.D.'s, M.B.A.'s, lawyers, and other top thinkers. We learned that our CFO had falsified corporate reports to cover an illegal act by the president, who had quickly resigned.

The new president studied the situation with the executive committee and announced that enough damage had occurred; there was no plan to sanction the CFO.

I suggested that this was not an appropriate response.

Our new leader said that she was afraid that firing "would reflect poorly on the institution." Others added that "our first obligation was to the institution"—a thinly disguised pitch for a cover-up. Here was their coda: "The CFO is a nice person, and I think he's learned his lesson."

But the CFO had breached his highest fiduciary duty—to tell the financial truth to the institution. He had also busted his C.P.A. oath by cooking the books. He had done the one thing he should not do.

Inside each of us is a great wrestling match between the desire to be just like everyone else and the call to be a separate—and potentially ostracized—individual. I hated to stand out. But Tony, my schools, and my mentors had tried earnestly to install core values in me. So I stated to the board that I no longer trusted or had confidence in the CFO. I said I was disappointed in the president and the executive committee's decision. I was immediately criticized.

"Gus, think of the damage that'll do to the institution!" said one of my colleagues. "Where's your compassion?" asked another. I felt the fear in the room and understood it but didn't want to ride its wave. Individual board members with great intelligence and experience pulled me aside to change my mind. As a compromise, the other members then voted to withhold the CFO's bonus. I was asked to remain the "unique [ethical] voice in a choir of many talented voices."

Professor Stephen L. Carter of Yale Law School tells us that compromises that advance high principles are acceptable; those that do not advance high principles are not.[2] Withholding a reward for outright lying and cheating was not a good compromise because it did not advance a principle. Instead, it covered a wrong, violated integrity, and lacked courage.

Nor do I advocate that boards designate a singleton ethical voice to speak for conscience. The board has a collective, fiduciary duty of conscience that cannot be delegated to one person. Because of what I perceived as an institutional failure of high core values, I resigned.

## Core Values

Everyone has core values. We live them in our actions, decisions, and relationships, and we display them publicly when we're under pressure. Admirable or not, a core value is a nonnegotiable practice that is most obvious in times of stress. Some core values are excellent, many are venal, and most are neither because they are often a little of both.

Some firms, such as Kimberly-Clark, promote a high core value such as *integrity* and actually live up to it. Institutional core values reflect the personal core values of the organization's leadership, and

Jim Collins traced those values back to the personal integrity of Darwin Smith, Kimberly-Clark's courageously backboned CEO.[3]

In my experience, most organizations state high or theoretical values for public consumption and then privately ignore them. Tyco's values, as it practiced historic grand larceny, were *integrity, excellence, teamwork*, and *accountability*. Sometimes companies advertise low values (such as naked profitability), but families, firms, and nations with low core values eventually fail. Enron followed its low core values, and those values killed the company.

Violent secession tested Lincoln's core value of *preserving the Union*; the result of that Point of Decision was an epic war of values and the modern United States. The deep fear of being cheated out of a national election tested another president's core value of *win at all costs*. The result was Watergate.

We see low core values when executives place a death grip on producing the appearance of quick results. We witness high core values when leaders hold fast to principled behaviors while they're being hammered for instant outcomes. Each places arms around his or her own personal, nonnegotiable values.

## Knowing Your Values

Where do we get our core values? Chris Kay, like most of us, formed them from experiences in early childhood, adolescence, young adulthood, career and professional life, and marital and parenting roles.

If you analyze Chris's iron-clad principles as he took the helm of his new company, you'd find *high personal integrity* and *conflict avoidance*. The first is a high core value; the second is not. Yet Chris knew his core values and assumed leadership with that insight.

Leaders and organizations must identify, name, and know their actual, operating core values. Those values will determine all results. When we know our personal and institutional core values, we can forecast our behaviors, particularly in times of stress.

When I was a new middle manager, I couldn't name my core values. If asked, I would've said, "I'm working on them." I was using an immature brew of instinct, impulse, and limited reflection. In retrospect, my values were *compassion, support,* and *integrity*. I had known great leaders but doubted my ability to emulate them. *Compassion,* my first—a medium value—continuously smacked into *integrity,* my third, which was a high value. I saw the results of the contradiction but didn't know how to resolve them. A person I liked would fail in performance, and my support and compassion would outvote my integrity.

This is because I knew I needed *integrity* but didn't understand the concept as I do now. There's a lot of that going around today. Journalists consistently write that our continuing scandals, corruption convictions, and business ethics challenges highlight the need for *honesty*.

Chris Kay had briefly considered *honesty* as an IntegWare core value. I asked him if Niles France, a troubled CEO we had known in the past, had been honest about wanting power and control.

"He was pretty clear about that," said Chris.

I told Chris that I had once prosecuted an ex-con who had promised to wipe out his neighbors because they had reported him.

The neighbors disliked the stink made by his garage meth lab, and the cops came. Later he made good on his word. This defendant told the truth. He wasn't good or admirable, but he was *honest*.

Analysis suggests that *honesty,* good as it is, lacks the height and depth to guide our best behaviors.

## Understanding Low, Middle, and High Core Values

It is important not only to identify your core values but also to recognize whether they are high, middle, or low.

### Low Core Values

Low core values are common habits. They are not best business practices. The behaviors of low core values can be found in all common organizations by the most unperceptive observer.

Yet people refuse to admit that they follow low core values. It's amusing that our low business values are desperately denied in public, openly criticized in the media, and popularly followed behind closed doors.

It's amusing, but it's not funny. These are the bad practices on the far side of the river of fear that sink spirits, kill morale, and cause corporations to tank.

These are the predatory omnivores that live within us, but seem too powerful for us to challenge, combat, or stop:

| | | | |
|---|---|---|---|
| abuse | appearances | arrogance | backstabbing |
| bigotry | bribery | cliques | control |
| cronyism | disrespect | egotism | expediency |
| favoritism | fear | gossip | greed |
| hostility | isolation | manipulation | misrepresentation |
| posing | pride | productivity | profits |
| puffery | racism | results | revenge |
| ruthlessness | sarcasm | self-interest | sexism |
| short-term planning | | | |

Low core values are seductive because they emerge from base human instincts and, if they don't result in lawsuits or consent decrees, can produce early, short-term results. They inevitably fail because they contravene the principles that invite and sustain true success and can't fulfill higher-order needs. This becomes obvious when top employees leave and customers become scarce.

Chris lived Hewlett-Packard's high core values during HP's era of wonder. In planning for IntegWare, he easily bypassed three of the low ones that, pursued for their own sake, lure so many of us: *productivity*, *results*, and *profits*. As Jim Collins says, profits are the results of great practices. They're not our reason for being but the consequences of applied high principles.[4]

## Middle Core Values

Middle core values are visible best business practices. Practiced purely, they are rare, but a good observer can see them in operation.

What's wrong with *best business practices*? Aristotle set the difference between the important and the essential; Jim Collins's research revealed the modern distinction: "Good is the enemy of great."[5] It sounds counterintuitive, but sustaining principles are actually greater than best practices.

Middle core values are *good* values. But they can seduce an executive or a corporation into thinking he or it has achieved genuine excellence. That's like looking at revenues and reading a 5 percent margin as 20 percent. For that vision-obscuring reason alone, middle core values are the inside enemies of great operating principles.

Middle core values are admirable and desirable, but they're only the *by-products* of high core values. Middle core values are produced by highest principles but are not principles themselves:

| | | | |
|---|---|---|---|
| customer focus | communication | compassion | consideration |
| creativity | development | diversity | duty |
| education | encouragement | ethics | excellence |
| innovation | honesty | honor | humility |
| leadership | learning | loyalty | quality |
| respect | service | support | teamwork |

For example, many have used "leadership" practices without integrity to produce catastrophe, making it a conditional quality.

"Chris," I said, naming a famous company, which I'll call Janways. "Janways has world-caliber leaders on its board, right?"

"Absolutely," he said.

"And it names *customer focus* as a nonnegotiable core value."

"Which is good," he said.

"You're right—it's *good*. But how does that core value affect Janways?"

"With *customer focus* as an operating principle, the firm recruits and advances execs that have customer-service passion."

"Which shows that Janways is aligned with its core value."

"Right! All looks *good*. But you know this'll happen: a customer under huge fourth-quarter pressure urges Janways execs to act illegally, hide losses, inflate revenues, hire a failing relative, cover an error, overlook shortfalls, or "fix" engineering data. It promises later benefits for immediate Janways contracts. *Customer focus* is nonnegotiable. What do these Janways execs do?

"They do the right thing. They say *no*. But I see what you mean. In Janways' culture, the customer—not principles—is number one. If you get a bad customer, you get to go down with him."

David Kai Tu, president of DCL, Inc., a $50 million-per-year high-tech firm, is one of the strongest yet humblest execs I know. Fearless in matters of integrity, he believes that courageous risk taking for character is no risk at all. A Chinese immigrant and master's-prepared engineer, David was once a young project manager for a general contractor.

One day, the president of a subcontracting firm gave David 50-yard-line tickets to watch his favorite NFL team play its key rival. David, built like a linebacker, was a four-sport athlete and is now a master golfer; in seconds, he had warmly accepted.

"As I was watching the game, I got to thinking—when not screaming my lungs out and downing Red Hots—*These are great tickets!* I realized that I was responsible for approving change orders from this subcontractor. I had to admit: these great seats could sway my perceptions toward the sub's position. *This generous offer had a price far beyond the value of the seats.* In the second quarter, I got up and left the game. From that Sunday forward, I made it my practice to not accept any offers from individuals or entities with whom I'd later have to make financial decisions. I didn't accept lunches or amenities such as vacations, cruises, resort stays, help with construction supplies or labor for my home from any contractors. Unusual practice in the construction trade, I later realized. When we set up our own company, we put high core values in on the ground floor."

"Right. That's Enron asking Arthur Andersen to hide losses in its wholly owned offshore entities. Boeing offering a top job to the Air Force procurement officer who reviewed Boeing's air tanker bid."

"So Janways," said Chris, "needs a high core value to make sure that customer focus doesn't unbalance the center."

Chris was exactly right. *Customer* focus—or any medium core value—can't be a core value without an accompanying high core value, such as *integrity*, to place it in operational context. Otherwise, it can unintentionally run the company off its rails, with publicly expensive results.

I asked Chris, "How about another middle core value: *teamwork*. Everyone wants teamwork. You've installed it. But as powerful and desirable as it is, it remains only a good value. Why do you think?"

He nodded. "I remember times when teamwork was used for wrong causes. For negative internal competition. Even for cheating."

"That's right! Teams are *unified power*. Power can be used for *anything*. But as a core value, it has to be enacted, come what may."

I once knew a team of highly talented global salespeople drawn from Fortune 50 firms. In a joint venture with a handsome Fortune 100 company, this team methodically embezzled millions through wrongful property acquisitions, faulty hires, fabricated financial records, and family junkets. These people—all friends—demonstrated the candor, communication, coordination, cooperation, consultation, and interdependence of a good team. But they were motivated by greed and larceny. The result: the venture failed, and all but one were fired. Their teamwork looked great. So do pirate crews until they're hanged.

In 2005, I met Jorge Valdes, a bright, charming, and well-spoken executive. He had once been the Medellin drug cartel's chief of U.S. operations. In that job, Valdes earned $1 million USD a month as he ruthlessly pursued his financial goals.

He told me that four behaviors made millionaires out of the cartel's tightly operated teams:

1. They were willing to die for their cause.
2. They were willing to die for each other.

3. They held common values.

4. They refused credit. (Taking credit would mean arrest, a federal indictment, and a possible life sentence.)

The downside? His team was murdered or imprisoned. Valdes was convicted in 1989 and faced eight consecutive life terms.

"My team lacked only one thing," he said. "*Principles*." Thus the men could make a killing until they were killed themselves.

A team is a unified force. It is no more inherently principled and admirable than the tides. In this distinction is the world of difference that separates *working hard* from *principle* and *good* from *great*.

It makes sense for an organization to adopt medium core values—but only if they are accompanied by at least one high core value.

## High Core Values

Great values suggest high core values. These are the highest principles. They are the platinum standard in a world that likes to trade in tin. History has tested these principles from ancient China and Greece through the age of Humanism to modern American capitalism. They have emerged enduring, sustaining, profitable, and heroic.

There are but three high core values:

Integrity          Courage          Character

Turn the heat up on each of these three values with blowtorch crises, flaming hazards, and off-the-cliff economic gymnastics, stress them with the flop-sweat, paper-curling need for instant results, and they remain pristine, powerful, and productive. Unlike medium core values, which can become weaknesses if pushed to extremes, you can push high core values harder, and they simply become stronger:

*Integrity. Courage. Character.* These are the biggest words in organizational theory. They should be used with discipline. That begins with understanding.

Business isn't football, but sports examples provide clear images. In 1979, the San Francisco 49ers had staggered through consecutive 2–14 seasons, had never won a championship, and were the NFL's doormat and a general embarrassment to pro sports. The new head coach, Stanford's Bill Walsh, had to improve the defense, which was playing like hippos on snowboards. Walsh changed the team's core value from *losing ugly* to *winning with excellence*. But when I read behind his systems, I see courage.

First, Walsh had the guts to accept the brutal truth. This meant risky reconstruction instead of staged reform. He then courageously applied his system of character hiring to assemble a staff and a team dominated by team players. The archetype analyst of talent, Walsh drafted three rookie defensive backs and traded for a top defensive end, an overage middle linebacker, and a safety that had spent the previous season clerking in a health foods store.[6] He saw their character, their selflessness, their commitment, and started them.

With thin, third-round backup quarterback Joe Montana, a no-name backfield and tenth-round receiver Dwight Clark, the West Coast offense scored points. The revamped defense placed second in the league, the team won sixteen games and the first Super Bowl it ever saw. An untested team of character had entered its Point of Decision and consistently beat teams with greater talent, speed, and experience.

At the beginning of this century, American business was reported to be the ethical doormat of international business. We earned this distinction by taking a fall from grace that has resembled a four-year-long nosedive. We remain in the headlights of an integrity failure that wiped out the retirement savings of two generations, lost $3 trillion in value, and won a worldwide F in business character.

To rebuild American business integrity, we must be as intentional about upgrading our principled practices as Bill Walsh was in building championship teams.

It starts with integrity, courage, and character.

# 3

# GOING DEEPER (AND HIGHER) INTO VALUES AND ETHICS

> By three methods we may learn wisdom: first, by reflection, which is noblest; second, by imitation, which is easiest; and third by experience, which is the bitterest.
>
> —*Confucius*

All too often, we Americans toss out words like *ethics*, *integrity*, and *character* as if they were interchangeable or as though we were discussing different grades of potatoes.

There is power in understanding the quality of each very different concept.

Let's consider integrity, courage, character, and ethics and examine the changes that we can enact when we see what separates them from each other.

## Integrity

Integrity is acting for what is right. When we do this, we feel whole and uniquely powerful.

*Integrity* comes from the Latin for "complete" and "incorruptible." Integrity has three parts:

1. Discern right from wrong.

2. Act for what is right regardless of risk to self.

3. Teach others from that act of integrity.[1]

In this very definition lives high human conduct.

Note that when we teach integrity, we exercise the essence of mentoring and coaching. They fulfill their purposes when exercised for principles. This is different from being a patron who advances careers, promotions, power, and wealth. Teaching integrity conveys character competence. This empowers us to live rightly instead of selfishly.

People follow courage and rightness from the heart.

That is why Chris Kay, who had lived this high definition at Hewlett-Packard, hoped that his new firm, IntegWare, would adopt *integrity* as one of its new core values.

In contemplating integrity, execs often ask, *How do you tell right from wrong?* Many believe that everything is relative. To show tolerance, we tend to see all viewpoints as correct. But this damages proven truths. When truth is unrecognized or ignored in business, the costs only begin in dollars.

Enron may have failed because of moral relativism, but make no mistake: its crash marked an absolute and total failure of integrity. We didn't need to consult with ten sharply discerning ethicists to understand that cheating is wrong and unbearably expensive.

Equally true is the sustained profitability of principled firms. But despite wisdom, education, and research, we struggle to *believe* it.

Fortunately, there are many paths to determining right from wrong. Our model has three parts.

1. Honor your conscience.
2. Question your prejudices and personal needs.
3. Consult wise counsel.

## Honor Your Conscience

The capacity for character resides in the deep circuits of our prefrontal cortex. Here also lives the conscience. Like Coach Tony made fighters, the conscience generates an innate sense of *moral rightness or blame* from actions. Having seen much corporate error, I believe we need to honor all red lights—particularly when they're our own.

Derived from the Latin word for the conscious knowledge of guilt, conscience holds the human sense of right and wrong, which is a fundamental survival tool. It is our point man, scouting out threats. The Hindus call it *dharmabuddhi* (moral wisdom) and *sadasadvichara shaki* (good-bad reflective power, or the "knowing voice of the soul"). The Hebrews linked it to the heart, which brings us full circle to Coach Tony's teachings about courage.

In English, Latin, Hindu, and Hebrew or in a boxing ring, conscience, when triggered by wrongful action, rings a mental bell and burns a bright red dashboard light that says, *Danger, Will Robinson.*

Children sense that warning. My own children, Jena and Eric, intentionally grew that capacity as teens. As adults, they, unlike me at their ages, are masters of knowing right from wrong.

Thus we begin in right and wrong by honoring our conscience.[2]

## Question Your Prejudices and Personal Needs

Honoring conscience is simple: you listen to yourself and watch for a blinking red light. But sometimes we don't get a clear signal; it flickers, fades, flickers again. This can happen when the fact pattern is very complex and our conscience is scanning heavy data.

This is the second step. It's a higher challenge because it means challenging yourself. Without a clear ruling from our conscience, where do we turn? We tend to rely on the comfortable and familiar, on our strongest core values. This is a terrific step if they're highly principled. But most of us have a broad range of value behaviors.

To have integrity, we are obligated to question ourselves as we would question any other data; it's time to put ourselves on the stand:

> *D.A.*: So you're in a values dilemma. No clear signal from your conscience, from the judicial side of your conscience?

> *Gus*: Right. No signal. I think we're in a gray area.

> *D.A.*: Isn't it true that "gray area" is a term we use to excuse what we want to do? You call it a gray area so you can do it without having to think about it anymore?

*Gus:* (adjusting his suddenly tight tie) Yes, and yes.

D.A.: So now you're turning to your actions to resolve the issue?

*Gus:* Sort of. I'm stuck. I'm really not taking action yet. That's why I called you in; you hold my values to figure out the hard stuff.

D.A.: OK. Here are my questions for you:

1. Which one gives you the easiest way out?
2. Which one makes you look the best?
3. Which one gives you more power or influence?
4. Which one serves your prejudices and biases?

*Gus:* Those are some pretty fierce questions.

D.A.: Well, I don't want to brag. They help you separate private belief and self-interest from principles and high values. So answer the questions candidly. It'll help you distinguish personal needs from acting rightly. Sometimes, they'll coincide. Many times, they won't. But this is testing the facts against your core values.

Find a place of quiet. Reflect on your answers. You may get a judicial indication, a red light. You may get a dim glow or nothing at all. But regardless, continued reflection will give a good sense of direction.

You're ready for the third step.

## Consult Wise Counsel

Consult with the most highly principled people you know. If you're living correctly, you're probably surrounded by them and you trust their counsel. Describe the facts, ask questions, and answer theirs. Listen well. You might even thank them.

Then run their counsel past your conscience. This should produce your answer from both conscience and reflection.

You have now dedicated major character muscle to discernment and are to be seriously commended. Congratulations!

Now all we have to do is act for what is right.

## Courage

This is the mental and moral strength to venture, persevere, and withstand danger, fear, or difficulty.

It comes from the Latin and Middle English word for "heart." Courage is the tip of the spear of integrity and the spark plug for principled conduct. It is integrity at its highest. This is because it faces fear, converts integrity into a habit, and gives enduring power and usefulness to leadership.

It is human behavior at its most admirable, selfless, and excellent. It is the stuff of epics, legends, and heroism. It is what we wish our children will possess and demonstrate. It is what we admire most in leaders, friends, and spouses.

Courage begins by facing strong negative, gut-wrenching feelings. It requires the direct and robust facing of fear.

Facing fear then becomes the correcting of internal wrongs and confronting, addressing, and correcting external wrongs in others.

As Coach Tony taught, this is an act of caring for others. The opposite of courage isn't fear; fear is simply the internal condition that courage overcomes. The opposite of courage is *indifference*. Courage comes from commitment, care, and love, whereas allowing wrongs in others leads to others' mistreatment and suffering.

That is why being *courageous* for rightness is superior to being "a good person" who keeps his own nose clean.

I was lucky in my teachers and coaches. I think we all were. The ones that persist deepest in memory didn't teach us skills; they taught us values. I see Tony's banged-up face, his thick Euro-stubble darkening as the day wore on. I can hear that deep, gruff New York accent. His whole life is telling me to have guts, to do right, to respect everyone whether I felt like it or not. He's telling me to face my fears, head up, backbone straight, my smile as ready as a quick left jab. He's telling me to follow up on what we did so that nothing bad happens to other people.

This rare action was the practice of several U.S. generations, which faced woes greater than layoffs and a loss of pensions and savings. Courage may not be an iconic behavior that we draw on from our daily screen savers. But if you understand our history, you know that this splendid capacity for courage is in our hard drives.

## Character

Character is the result of sustained integrity and courage. It derives from a Greek word that means "engrave, impress deeply and permanently." It is possessed by a person with fixed habits of moral firmness and excellence who acts spontaneously for what is right.

A person of character has consistently demonstrated the behaviors of courage and integrity over a lifetime.

But when we apply the highest-value word to those who frequently but inconsistently demonstrated courage or use it in other careless ways, the word *character* loses its meaning.

Character is the most challenging core value because it requires a lifetime to fulfill.

## Ethics

As an ethicist, the media ask me to comment on a breaking story and to declare if a described action is *ethical*. Ethics means to adhere to a code that governs professional or social conduct.

I say that there are two types of ethics: formal ethical codes that are published, and informal, internal ethical codes that reflect true corporate culture and practice, that is, actual core values.

Formal ethical codes can be purely theoretical. This means that informal, internal ethical codes have far more impact on actual behaviors.

Arthur Andersen's central core value used to be *accounting integrity*. Its formal and informal codes of ethics absolutely forbade misrepresentation of audit data. But under pressure, a new, informal core value evolved: *maximum revenues by whatever means.*

When more pressure made this value fully operational, the formal code died and the informal, cultural code became dominant. Arthur Andersen then created the perfect ethics storm of economic cannibalism when it provided services to Enron, a company with an informal, internal code of *high-risk deals and results at all costs.*

Enron execs who questioned Andersen's creative accounting were accused of not being "team players." The power of the informal code silenced voices that might have been courageous.

This teaches us three things: (1) Ethics is not right or wrong; it's just a code. (2) An ethics code is only as good as its sponsors' informal, cultural code of actual practice. (3) A gap between formal and informal codes can be institutionally and professionally fatal.

Thus ethics is a *good* word but not a *great* one. Ethics is situational and local to the practice and the institution or industry. It's *related* to character, but it is not character, which is about the self. *Ethics* is about rules and was never designed for the universal heavy lifting that is the specialized work of the great enduring principles.

Remember that intermixing high values like *courage* and *integrity* with middle values like *honesty* and *ethics* is like mistaking Curley of the Three Stooges for Meryl Streep because they're both actors.

We now see the difference between high, medium, and low core values. We know that all values aren't the same and that what we select is crucial not only to creating sustained success but to avoiding catastrophe.

People use the word *ethics* as the end-all and be-all, but now you and I know that it merely refers to a code of behavior. Yet there are powerful codes of ethics. Section 3.6 of the 2001 American Nurses Association Code of Ethics directs nurses to report impaired practice by colleagues. This represents codified integrity (acting for what is right regardless of risk) and courage (correcting wrongs regardless of danger).

Similarly, Section 14 of Army Regulation 600-50 requires military personnel to report violations of standards of conduct.[3] In these two respects, it's not enough to refrain from corrupting the water supply; as a professional, you're obligated to report the corruptions of others.

Few corporate ethics codes require reporting of wrongs. For example, a famous CEO helped his company promulgate a well-known code of ethics. He then openly breached three of its central values. Yet no one inside his very large company reported his acts.

Despite appearances, the code was inherently weak. Why? Because from the outset it tolerated ethical breaches by others.

A bright friend of mine was a senior exec in this major firm. I asked him what he thought of his CEO's unethical actions, which had been reported in the business press and by the SEC after its levying of a massive fine for his inflating corporate profits.

My friend said, "Gus, the man made me rich. I can't complain."

This is the tension between core values and results. We see the evidence that high core values gives us sustained profits. But then we see cheaters make gains. This, most illogically, makes us feel like rejecting high core values, despite our sure knowledge that a lack of principles kills trust, relationships, families, and profits. We see the writing on the wall but struggle to believe it.

Until we trust our head and rely on our heart's courage, our principles and core values, like my friend's, will remain for sale.

Imagine a day in which every decision you make is based on the high core values of integrity, courage, and character, and it will be so. Imagine a team in which all interactions are intentionally designed to be principled and courageous, and that will be so as well.

## Crossing the River: Seeking Core Values

Put a strip of yellow crime scene tape on the floor. Ask a representative group of 50 U.S. executives to divide into "good people" to the left of the tape and "courageous people" to the right.

The good people are honest; they don't cheat or steal and seldom cause serious problems. But they don't solve the tough moral ones, either. This suggests that such people cannot effectively lead.

The courageous stand to the right. They boldly take risks for principles and for others. Out of fifty managers, you can count the members of this group on one hand.

A river separates our two groups of execs (see Figure 3.1). The tape dividing the groups represents the River of Fear.

**Figure 3.1.  A "River of Fear" Separates Good Executives from Courageous Ones**

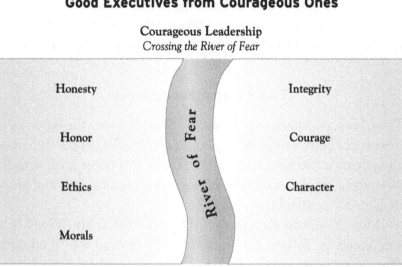

Courageous Leadership
*Crossing the River of Fear*

| Honesty | | Integrity |
| Honor | River of Fear | Courage |
| Ethics | | Character |
| Morals | | |

For many of my forbears in Shanghai, Yangzhou, and Suzhou, their greatest fear was being *kong hsu*, socially disconnected and abandoned by the *jia*, the clan. Being isolated in a relational society feels like death.

For most American businesspeople, our night fears have to do with conflicts, bad feelings, negative emotions, confrontation, getting fired, and people not liking us.

It is not so unlike being *kong hsu*.

The River of Fear deals with feelings—what some of us would call "touchy-feely" concepts. Yet fear of feelings is strong enough to act as a barrier that separates the good from the courageous and splits the hesitant from the bold and the quietly heroic.

In memory, I see my coach pulling two fighters apart. One kid, a street punk who likes to spit in the soup and shoulder-bump little kids, is behind on points. His blood up, terrified of losing, he swings at his opponent as they come out of the clinch; this is a clear foul and a dirty, cheap-shot violation of the Rules of Queensbury.

"*Hey!*" shouts Tony. "Don't disgrace yourself!"

In that moment, I realize that Tony cares for the punk as much as he cares for any of us. It's humbling in its instruction. Of the few things Tony hated—cowardice, violating the rules, and indifference to other people—I think he hated indifference to oneself even more.

## The Character Matrix

The Character Matrix (see Figure 3.2) demonstrates the behavioral differences between good people and courageous people. It makes clear that the two constitute distinctly different tribes, each with its own strongly reinforced core values and cultural habits and practices, as different as bison and fish.

Most American managers belong on the left, in the "Good Person" category. Talk to American HR experts and they'll confirm that the vast majority of male executives don't cheat but are conflict-averse. Most of these experts will estimate the number of the avoidant in times of conflict to be about 80 percent.

### Figure 3.2.  The Character Matrix

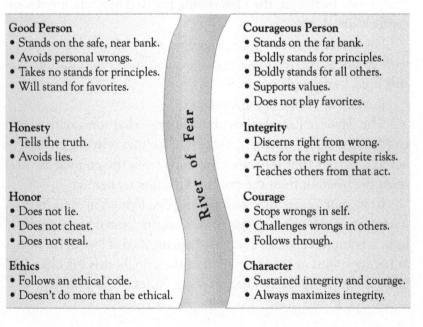

**Good Person**
- Stands on the safe, near bank.
- Avoids personal wrongs.
- Takes no stands for principles.
- Will stand for favorites.

**Honesty**
- Tells the truth.
- Avoids lies.

**Honor**
- Does not lie.
- Does not cheat.
- Does not steal.

**Ethics**
- Follows an ethical code.
- Doesn't do more than be ethical.

*River of Fear*

**Courageous Person**
- Stands on the far bank.
- Boldly stands for principles.
- Boldly stands for all others.
- Supports values.
- Does not play favorites.

**Integrity**
- Discerns right from wrong.
- Acts for the right despite risks.
- Teaches others from that act.

**Courage**
- Stops wrongs in self.
- Challenges wrongs in others.
- Follows through.

**Character**
- Sustained integrity and courage.
- Always maximizes integrity.

Notably, most of them agree that American female executives are more courageous in approaching conflict but often lack the institutional authority to have the impact of their male counterparts.

What's paradoxical is that the overwhelming majority of us don't want to think of ourselves as cowardly.

We want to be courageous people, but we think the river, which separates the two sides of the matrix, stops us.

Of course, this is inaccurate. What stops us is ourselves.

We are also discouraged and disheartened because we don't have specific river-crossing tools that would increase our chances for long-term success after we've overcome our fears.

This book allows us to see the consequences of trying to play it safe.

More important, it equips us to cross the river.

First, let's examine the behaviors that create two asynchronous American business tribes.

We all want high core values that will align our companies, our organizations, and our lives, with sustained success. Knowing that everyone operates from a private set of core values helps us begin the process of intentionally choosing our own with great care.

We begin by honestly assessing the actual, applied core values we've used to operate. If they are not high values, we have a golden opportunity to upgrade them.

Let's watch, in Chapter Four, as Chris Kay begins consciously aligning his behaviors with the high core values he has always admired and wanted.

# 4

# CHRIS BOLDLY MOVES FORWARD

You gain strength, courage, and confidence by every
experience in which you really stop to look fear in
the face.

*—Eleanor Roosevelt*

Chris Kay's childhood heroes were Batman, because of his great
gadgets, and Superman, because he had the power to do anything
and used it to fight crime. When so many kids followed the Yan-
kees, Chris became a Cowboys and Roger Staubach fan. The
attachment deepened when Chris, while still quite young, learned
that his favorite team's quarterback was a great family man. As
Chris grew into adulthood, he didn't lose his interest in technology,
his commitment to fighting for what is right, or his admiration for
courageous family loyalty.

Chris would need those attachments to solve his next challenge, for Will Sampson was appropriately named. His big frame,
clown-wide shoulders, and booming midwestern voice with a Henry
Fonda twang were summed up in a neon sign that said *supersized*
and *focused*. His mind was agile and his manner was warm, welcoming, and disarming. If he didn't get you with charm, he could
catch you with mental quickness.

Chris has a lot of backbone. He resolved to continue seeking
accord with his influential COO.

"Will," said Chris, "how are you doing?"

"Chris, I'm great! How are you? And your beautiful family?"

"We're all fine, thanks. How's your uncle?"

"Chris," said Will in his reliable tones, "good of you to ask. You know that since my wife's Uncle Henry moved in, our home has been turned upside down. He hasn't been able to find work. Until he does, he needs a place to live. Now it turns out he needs an exercise program. He has an appointment at a local gym right after lunch, and I'm the only one who can take him."

"That's good that you can help. I'm sorry about the complications to your family. Will, I need your plan for core values development by 6 P.M. today."

"I'm sorry, Chris." A sad smile. "I'm going to be tied up all afternoon."

"When can you get it to me?"

"By Friday. Thanks, Chris, for understanding. You're the best."

Chris was being affirmative and could feel that he was on task.

The problem was that Will Sampson stymied Chris's intentionality by subtly using his need for accord against him. Sampson knew that Chris loved optimum productivity and loathed bickering, so he verbally acknowledged Chris's concerns while promising better performance. Chris could leave these meetings and check the block that said "Have tough conversation with Sampson." But it was puzzling; he was swinging mightily at a half-burned tree, but no chips were flying.

"Gus," said Chris, "you said that courage is an expression of caring. That if we care, we then have the guts to act."

"I couldn't have said it better," I replied.

"Well, it's not working. I care about Will. The guy drives me nuts, but I care about him and his family, and that's why I can't fire him."

"Chris, if I hired you to rewire our phone systems and you simply couldn't do it, would I be showing care by keeping you on?"

"Of course not. You saying compassion's not a good thing?"

"That might be it. Is there anything higher than compassion?"

"I'm sure there is. Well, you know I hate conflict."

"Almost all of us do. Why do you think *you* hate it?"

Chris remembered his parents' inability to cope with conflict. Rather than face hard feelings, his father had left their home.

"I learned to fear conflict," he said. "I associate conflict with the most powerfully negative possible outcomes." *Divorce, sadness, loss. Lying awake at night, wrestling with bad feelings.*

"Chris, those are incredibly powerful forces. How do you think you could stop them from influencing your behaviors?"

"Well, heck, if I knew that, what would I need you for? Come on—no more questions. Tell me what you think I should do."

I laughed. "When your parents couldn't solve conflicts, they divorced. If you can't solve the conflicts with Sampson, Stingley, and Dornier Klein, what'll happen?"

"IntegWare loses its chance at greatness. Maybe at surviving."

"I agree. Now tell me the real cost if you confront Sampson. I mean, *really* confront him. Tell him that you expect him to initiate core values work with the entire firm by Friday and fix the Stingley-Klein issue by the following Friday, or you're letting him go."

"He could quit and take people with him. Gene Stingley could quit and we lose Dornier Klein. But I'd have the company back."

"Exactly. The famous British General William Slim said, given two equal options, take the bolder one.[1] That's because one, courage is a high value, and two, because leadership requires it. Just tell each of these parties the truth. What's the truth with Will Sampson?"

"The truth? That he worries me, puzzles me, frustrates me. He's putting us in jeopardy."

"I remember you said to me, 'My COO, Will Sampson. International IBM experience. Top schools. Very, very smart. Great presence. And he's killing me.' That's what you need to say to him."

"What if he quits?" asked Chris.

"Then your problem is solved."

"And if he takes people with him?"

"You'll hire better folk. People who won't follow Will Sampsons."

"And Gene Stingley? What about him and Dornier Klein?"

"Chris, I sense you're reluctant to talk to a guy who's hard to talk to and who's said that discussing his relationship with Klein is off limits.

"With Sampson, you've been overly supportive and conflict-avoidant. With Stingley, you've just been conflict-avoidant. What would happen if you were direct and truthful with both?

"What if you told Sampson he's killing you? And held his feet to the performance fire? That's the right thing."

"And if he doesn't perform?"

"Then you have another opportunity to do the right thing. What if you told Stingley that you need him? Created a principled relationship with him? What do you lose if you take him to lunch and listen? What if you were a spellbinding listener with him?"

"Hard to imagine," said Chris. "He hardly talks."

"This is a chance to get to know him. He's brilliant. As a leader, you find every person fascinating. You can encourage. Gene works for *you*, not Dornier Klein. The CEO before you let Stingley, a great independent spirit, fly solo. You want to change that?"

"Funny," said Chris. "I hate dealing with problems like this. Human conflict." He shook his head. "But I love these people. I love the idea of what this company can be. I really do."

"I know you do. And is that love greater than your fear?"

He nodded. "Yes, it is," he said.

"Then you're ready to reshape your relationship with Will Sampson. Instead of using his delaying tactics, you can deploy doing the right thing. You can use *courage*. You can show your *character*."

"Just face my conflict aversion and talk to the guy."

"That's right. You're equipped. You have the tools. Remember that you believe passionately in principled conduct. You're not doing this for you—you're doing it for the people in your company and for the people who rely on your people. And even for Will Sampson."

"OK," said Chris. We reviewed a specific course of action. He rehearsed. He conferred with his lawyer and began recording Will Sampson's promises of performance on his deliverables. A month passed without any improvement by Will.

Chris then met Will Sampson off campus.

"What's up, Boss?" asked Sampson cheerfully. They shook hands.

"Will, how are you doing?" asked Chris warmly.

"Not bad, thanks for asking."

"How's your Uncle Henry?" Chris always asked because the issue seemed very important to Will and his family.

"Doing fine." Will again explained in detail the need to have his wife's healthy and unemployed uncle live with them.

"This is a responsibility on you and Adele," said Chris.

"It is, thank you for seeing that."

"Will, how could I have supported you better during this time?"

"I have no complaints," said Will.

"Will, can we talk about the company's core values project? Do you know how badly I need that done for the firm?"

Will smiled wryly. "Of course I do. You tell me every other damn day that you need 'em to get everyone aligned on the same sheet of music." Will said it deeply, a distant warning, with a grin to ease the threat. Left jab, a feigned right cross.

"How much more time do you need to launch the project?" Chris pulled out his planner to emphasize his seriousness.

Will sighed. "Not much. I'm nearly done."

"Will, that's great! That's a big relief to me. How much more time do you want?"

Will sighed tiredly. "A day or two. No more than a week. Don't you get tired of asking me?"

Chris wrote down Will's words. "That's great. That means it'll be launched by the seventh of the month. Is that a deal?"

"I'll get it done, Chris. No need to keep hounding me."

"Yes, I hear that. You've got to be tired of hearing my concerns. Let me ask you this—do you feel you know my standards of execution? Of what's 'IntegWare-acceptable' in our ops?"

"Of course, Bucko. I sent the memo. I'm not sure why you're asking me this. I think you also know I've been in a bit of a family fix."

"I appreciate that. I care a lot about you and your family. Do you know how much time I've effectively given you to not produce?"

"A fair space," said Will. "Which I've appreciated."

"I'm glad. Will, it's actually been over four months. How much more time do you think I should allocate for nonproduction?"

"Not much longer." He pushed back from the table. "I resent your term, *nonproduction*. I've just been a little behind."

"I'm sorry for that. I'm looking at six deliverables, three of which were overdue to my predecessor before I joined the firm in June. Will, you promised that the core values project would launch last month. Then two weeks ago. Then last Friday. When I think of these blown deadlines, I'm very disappointed."

"Whoa!" said Will loudly. "No need to get personal!"

"Will, what happens in IntegWare *is* personal to me. I'm hoping that it'll be personal to you, too. Can you do that? Join me in this?"

"Listen, Chris, I'm with you. Stop playing rah-rah with me."

"OK, Will. I'll do that." Chris opened his briefcase and drew out a sheet of paper. "That time now ends. Effective now, I'm instructing you to have a complete and *acceptable* project execution plan for company core values development on my desk by 6 P.M. Friday. I'm handing you a statement of work that describes that deliverable." He handed it to Will, who began reading it. "You'll find it's wholly consistent with our previous talks and e-mails on this project."

Will put down the paper. He spoke deliberately, as if Chris had a head injury or a language problem. "You're wrong. This looks quite different. On the whole, it's a quite unreasonable work request."

Chris forced himself to not furrow his brow into the Marianas Trench. Openly, he said, "I disagree. You've told me four times you're nearly done. You now have a full additional week just to polish it."

Will leaned forward, smiling warmly. "Chris, we say a lot of things when we're under pressure." His eyes teared and his voice broke from genuine internal anguish, making Chris's heart pause.

"My wife's uncle needs our help. I'm afraid it's affecting our marriage. You have no idea of the stress. I tried to do a good thing, and it's not working. Honestly, I need more time."

Chris clenched his jaw to stop himself from saying, *OK, Will, take as long as you need.* He had rehearsed and said, "I'm so sorry, Will. That has to be very painful. I have no more time to give you."

Chris paused, looking into Sampson's eyes, and smiled warmly. "You're strong and gifted. I'm counting on your ability to help your family and to help me save a terrific company. I need the plan Friday."

"And if I can't manage that?"

"Then I'll be disappointed. I'll have to quickly find a COO who can deliver what the company so desperately needs."

Will Sampson took a deep breath, expanding his chest cavity and swelling his wide shoulders. The prognathous jaw jutted and his dark eyes narrowed. Chris thought of a Texas bobcat in a net. Sampson's deep voice sounded like desert meat grinder.

"Listen. I've seen crap before. No one talks to me like this." He showed his teeth, as if he had a primitive, feral grip on his job.

"I hear you," said Chris calmly. "I'm sorry you feel that way. Nothing you can say will stop me from respecting you and caring for you. This isn't easy for either of us. You getting the deliverable done—that's easy."

Will shook his head. "You can't run me out."

"No one's worked harder to keep you in," said Chris. He offered his hand. Will considered, then languidly shook Chris's hand

"I'm not so easy to fire," he muttered at Chris.

"I look forward to your good work." Chris thanked him and left.

Friday came and left without the execution plan showing up on Chris's desk or e-mail.

Chris met Will in the executive conference room. He greeted Will warmly, asked how he was, and respectfully offered him a separation agreement with a severance package, a good benefits feature, and a buy-out. Will challenged, argued, protested, and then tried to delay.

"Will," said Chris, "I regret to tell you, this is your last day. As I told you, every day that you delay in signing the package results in a reduction of benefits. Please leave your keys at reception."

Will stood close to Chris. "You can't do this to me."

Chris stood. Will towered over him. "Will, I am very sorry. You're released from this company, effective now."

Will's jaw almost pushed into the top of Chris's head. Chris felt a jolt of alarm and courageously stood his ground. Looking at Will frankly, he breathed steadily and slowly.

"You'll regret this!" snarled Will. "You'll hear from my lawyer!"

"Good-bye, Will, and good luck," said Chris.

I asked Chris how he felt.

"Relieved! The bad feelings I had firing him were nothing compared to the fears I had when I was letting Will drift along. I know I'm going to sleep better tonight than I have in months."

A few days later, Chris walked into Gene Stingley's office.

"Good morning," said Chris to Gene.

Stingley resembles Robert Oppenheimer, the atomic bomb scientist—tall, reserved, spare, and almost bursting with brains. Gene set his own hours, often working at home. He was reviewing a requirements package and barely acknowledged Chris's greeting.

"Gene, I'm sorry for the delay in meeting with you. You're one of our top thinkers and producers. As a result of your professionalism, you earned a special relationship with a top client. That top client has kept us alive recently. Please accept my profound thanks."

Gene shifted in his Herman Miller chair. He thought for a moment and made a small face of surprise. "Thanks," he said quietly.

"Thank *you*, Gene. I have a lot to learn about this firm from you. Would you be willing to schedule a lunch so I can get started?"

"Don't need to do that," said Gene.

"I can't agree. You're too important. Please, Gene."

Chris chose a restaurant with a private room. He served coffee for both of them and ordered quickly. Gene took several minutes.

"Thanks for your time," said Chris. "The firm owes you a great deal. I know you're well compensated, so I'm talking about recognition. People showing they care about you and what you've done."

"That's never mattered."

"Tell me more about that."

He shrugged a shoulder. "I've lived fine without it."

"You are very independent, a self-starter. Gene, I want to hold a company celebration when we finish this cycle. Could I briefly recognize you then?"

Gene Stingley shook his head. He was frowning.

"Then can I continue to thank you in private?"

"If you need to."

"I need to. Thanks."

Gene nodded, studying the menu from which he had already ordered and looking meaningfully at his watch.

"Coffee's hot and we have privacy. Eaten here before?"

Gene paused his reading to shake his head. He sipped coffee.

"You have an MIT Ph.D. Ever meet President Susan Hockfield?"

Gene shook his head.

"She looks to be very impressive."

Silence.

Chris thought of the story about the famously silent Calvin Coolidge. "Mr. President," said a White House dinner guest. "I bet a friend of mine that I could get you to say more than two words to me this evening." The president looked straight at her and said, "You lose."

"Gene—what's your life dream? What do you hope to do that you haven't already done?"

Gene dropped the menu like Sampson downing his work order, clearing the deck before torching the boss. "That's private," he said.

"I'm sorry." *Be authentic*, he reminded himself. "Looks like I'm having trouble connecting with you."

"It happens."

"To me, too," said Chris with a grin. "Sometimes I'd rather crunch numbers. But I feel bad that I seem to be striking out with you."

"So why not drop the small talk and get to the point?"

"All right, Gene, I will." He leaned forward. "Part of the point was trying to get to know you. And knowing how I can best support you."

"Really. You want to know how to support me? *Leave me alone.* You didn't have to drag me to lunch to figure that out."

Chris nodded. *This is as much fun as trapping a mad skunk. Just stand in the pocket; stay with him. Keep using the tools. Don't quit.*

"I can see," said Chris methodically, "how that might be easier on both of us in the short run. But I'm thinking long-term."

"Well, it's your job to do that, isn't it?"

"Absolutely! Gene, you see solutions others don't. You own a crucial relationship. To make IntegWare work, I need your help."

"So this lunch isn't about thanking me. It's about helping you."

Chris smiled and agreed. "I hear what you're saying. You're right—our meeting has a lot of different meanings. Including helping me."

Their food came. Chris was hungry, but he ignored his platter. Gene picked at his meal, looked out the window, and checked the time.

"We can go back to the office if you want," said Chris. He held his breath and smiled ever so slightly.

Gene thought it over. "Nah, let's at least eat."

They ate. Gene answered messages while he chewed. They had ten minutes of silence. In American business culture, that's the equivalent of two galactic eternities. In Asia, it's a moment between bites.

Gene pushed back his platter. "I don't want to be COO."

"OK. Can you tell me why?" asked Chris, heartened that Gene had opened a genuine topic on his own.

Gene shrugged. "Dornier Klein pushed the idea because they don't like how I'm being treated."

"That's a great compliment, a client going to bat for you and offering a position in their firm. So how *are* you being treated?"

"OK for now. But I know what you want. You want to horn in on my relationship with Klein. And you're not too excited about my setting my own hours."

"I'm glad you're OK for now with how you're treated. You're right—I'm concerned about Klein. But I don't want to horn in. That would damage your relationship to them, and your relationship with them is all IntegWare has. Gene, I've seen your product. You outwork everyone. My long-term concern is you might be working too hard."

Gene looked up and stared at Chris like a kid checking out a parent who told him he'd be getting a car for Christmas.

"Really."

"Really," said Chris. "So let me sum up. Two things I can do to support you is not hurt your relationship with Klein and leave your hours alone."

"Are we done?" asked Gene.

"If you want. Your hours are your own."

"You want more time with me?" asked Gene. Chris nodded. Gene sighed. He shook his wrist and lifted his eyebrows: *What else?*

"I feel like you're not telling me stuff that I need to know."

Gene's eyes bore into Chris's. "You know I had a special arrangement with your predecessor."

"No, I didn't know that."

Gene looked away, the eye contact too much for him. "The old CEO let me have my own patents."

Chris's eyebrows rose. "A remarkable special arrangement. Is it important to you to have patent ownership?"

"I expect you to not change things."

"Let me talk to my predecessor and get back to you on that."

"OK. Don't disappoint me."

"I'll try not to. But everything's a balance, wouldn't you agree?"

"Depends how it turns out."

Chris paused. "You matter to me, Gene. I want you to know that."

Gene leaned back. "You getting touchy-feely with me?"

"No. I'm being truthful. You matter. What you do matters to me. It also matters to others. How you treat others matters to me."

"You want me to be nice to you because you're new?"

Chris smiled. "Sure I would. But I want you to be as principled with me and everyone else as you are with your work."

"That's never mattered before."

"You're right. You've seen things. How would you judge the consequences of the company not valuing principled relationships?"

"You saying the firm's in trouble because of that?"

"It could be. What would you blame for our troubles?"

"Easy," said Gene. "Lack of vision. No strategic planning. Poor spending habits. Probably some mistakes in borrowing. Weak sales work. Lack of leadership. No teamwork. See, technical things."

Chris nodded. "That's the list. I'm with you on that."

"So what's this thing about *relationships?*"

"Good question! Gene, does our lack of vision connect in any way to how people have related to each other in IntegWare?"

Gene Stingley blinked as he saw something. "The ones with vision don't relate to the people who think tactically. Same with our planning, or lack of it. And spending. Of course, leadership, teams . . . ."

He saw that people weren't in relationship and that they didn't communicate. Knowledge remained in isolated niches.

"You can see," said Chris, "why it's the likeliest suspect I got."

"What are you really after with me?" asked Gene.

"I want a good professional relationship with you."

"No offense, but I don't think we'll ever be friends."

"We don't need to be. We just need to be colleagues and teammates. Friends are more, I think, for our private lives."

Gene almost smiled. A pause. "Thanks for lunch."

Work culture improved with Sampson's departure and Chris's evolving, principled relationship with Gene and others. IntegWare had witnessed Chris modeling integrity by taking the hits of no pay and longer hours for his people; of facilitating an open and consultative core values identification process for the company; of using teamwork and a character filter to hire principled and courageous new staff; of fulfilling customer requirements, needs, and wishes; and of making some progress, although slight, to create a better work-life balance.

Chris kept meeting with his people, including Gene Stingley. In the fall, Gene invited Chris to Dornier Klein's sales conference. The company's law firm continued to meet with Will Sampson's lawyer, who accepted IntegWare's small final offer.

Before the company paid off all its debts, before it received a primary unsecured line of credit, and before his new IntegWare team posted a 24.5 percent net profit, Chris found himself in the kitchen before dinner. It was spring, and sunlight flooded the house. His family looked at him the way families did in World War II films when the veteran comes home—marveling, smiling, mouths agape, stunned. It had been months since they had seen him before 8 P.M.

He kissed Janet and the kids and then hugged Heather and Grant, who held onto his legs as if they were life itself.

"How was practice, Heather?" he asked.

"Great," she said, so happy to see him.

He turned to his son. "Hey, Grant. *Wanna rassle?*"

"You bet, Dad!" cried Grant, growling like a bear cub, trying to pull his father down to earth. Although Chris is very solid, his small son was magically able to topple him. With a great whoop, Grant jumped all over his dad, and childlike laughter filled the house as Heather jumped onto the pile. Chris is fortunate in many ways, both seen and unseen. This moment, however, was pure sweetness.

Chris Kay has shown us how to cross the river. By using the behavioral skill sets that you will learn in Part Two, he has begun the turnaround his company needs. He began that process by leveraging his already considerable leadership abilities with an intentional acquisition of competencies required by his new position.

There is no mystery that the conscious improvement of Chris's corporate leadership has also led to a parallel commitment as a parent and spouse.

By deliberately embracing the personal core values of integrity, courage, and character, he has upgraded everything he does.

# 5

# CODA: APPLYING COURAGEOUS VALUES AT WHIRLPOOL

The great need for anyone in authority is courage.
—*Alistair Cooke*

Mike Thieneman looked for sunshine. Through the windows of Whirlpool's administration building, he gazed at a Lake Michigan winterscape created by a glassy January snowfall. It was a snow that cloaked tall pines and billowed over the vast white lake to freeze great Chicago on the far shore. For a moment, the snow revived the fading and momentary magic of Christmas.

It reminded Thieneman of a small but dynamic Kentucky truck garden and bedding plants that he, the firstborn son of nine very poor kids, nurtured through good seasons and bad. Such a snow had made his father's night job-leaps from moving boxcars riskier as he switched trains on the second shift in the Louisville rail yards.

But the whiteness could not cover the sharp pain of Christmas, when the high joy of family and season had been diluted by the sadness of broken promises. When people in the company you love disappoint you, the pain goes to the heart.

Whirlpool is a Fortune 200 company with a good name, a fine line of products, and over seventy thousand employees around the globe. It is the world's largest manufacturer and marketer of home appliances. The winter lake scene was breathtaking, but on this day, to Mike Thieneman, Whirlpool was not a pretty place. Thus began a Senior Executive meeting on January 3.

"How was the holiday, Mike?" asked Chairman Dave Whitwam.

Mike Thieneman is a tall, thoughtful man with manners from a more civil era and a mind that could fence with Einstein. He has a Ph.D. in physics with two other graduate degrees, but he had to think hard. Thieneman takes integrity seriously. But he lied. "OK," he said.

He and the other senior executives took seats in the North Board Room, a ponderous space appropriate to one of America's last major domestic metal-bending manufacturers. A great, dark mahogany conference table with twenty chairs sits under the ominous and haunting scrutiny of the corporation's five former CEOs. Appearing as disembodied portraits, they still seemed prepared to vote.

The meeting began. Accustomed to good years, Whirlpool had missed its profit mark by a wide margin, close to $100 million. The Executive Committee had known this before Christmas.

But instead of isolating the root cause of the miss, this talented and experienced global executive group had fallen into blaming, finger-pointing, and self-protection throughout the preceding months.

Mike Thieneman was in a hard spot. Most of the revenue losses could be tracked to dramatic increases in material costs, and he ran global procurement. Over a year ago, Thieneman, and many others lower in rank, had fired loud warnings across the breadth of the company about the inevitability of rising costs.

In succeeding quarters, they again announced that materials costs were going to skyrocket well beyond original estimates.

"The issue," Thieneman said to the table, "is that we didn't listen to the troops. We wouldn't face reality. We denied truth. That's not how we're supposed to operate. It's not how we're supposed to be. I'm asking us to take responsibility for that so we can begin repairs."

The truth had arrived early in the form of warnings, which were disregarded for any number of human reasons. The truth formally returned as missing profitability at the end of the year.

It was then that some of the people who had not listened earlier showed the conventional forms of cowardice that I knew intimately:

They hid. They blamed others. They said, "It's not my fault."

An organization approaching a Point of Decision—a crisis between high and low values—must act bravely or buckle seat belts for a moral meltdown. There are no other choices.

That cold January, Whirlpool's top execs could have tried to avoid the pain by denying the evidence. The committee could ignore, criticize, or even jettison the people calling for a courageous response.

Or it could move those who had not listened, had ignored warnings, and were now blaming others and claiming no responsibility.

The initial response to the discussion was to blame every possible factor of design, production, marketing, sales, and delivery. There were calls for firings, reassignments, and revamps.

"We came very close to cracking and breaking," Mike Thieneman told me. "We had hard dialogue. Heated discussions. Emotion. But executives who do not face and react to reality have to be moved."

Whirlpool had arrived at its Point of Decision with more than annual earnings at stake; on the table also sat its very soul.

If you possessed excellent strategic vision and an understanding of people, you would have seen, on that long, elegant table, a high test of backbone and, ultimately, the supreme power of courage over fear.

Chairman David Whitwam is a gentle, dignified leader. He looks like a wise, compassionate, unassuming Dutch uncle in a country fable. But what he says, quietly but firmly, has the power of howitzers. Long before, he had explained to his executives his view of good fortune.

"I was very lucky. When I first arrived at Whirlpool, Bill Mahron (then the president) said to me, 'This is a company where if you lose ten million, we'll sit you down and we'll talk. But if you steal a hammer . . .'"

Dave was telling the troops that truth and courage lived personally in his heart. He was saying you can make or lose money, but don't mess with our high core values, for our integrity is our true life blood. It's the stuff that makes the money.

Now, in the board room, facing the emotion, the blaming, the lack of unified focus, the crescendo of intellectual energy and emotional disturbance, Dave Whitwam spoke quietly, firmly, clearly:

"Look, we can't continue to operate this way. It's bad enough to miss targets. Worse, the fabric of the company is being torn. If we don't recognize the issue, the tear could be repeated and the damage can worsen. The point is that there is no right way to do a wrong thing."

At Whirlpool, at a time of painful self-questioning and self-examination, Mike Thieneman, Dave Whitwam, and others played the courage card at the Point of Decision.

It was the best thing they did.

After-action reviews (AARs) are structured debriefings that analyze what actually happened in an event. AARs call for a fearless assessment of lessons learned and an identification of needed education and training for subsequent operations.

It's not a performance evaluation of individual executives or a witch hunt. Instead, it's an objective and disciplined analysis of the organization at work with a particular task and human and material resources. The best AARs are conducted in strategic alignment with high core values instead of with immediate results. Whirlpool, on the third day of a new year, did such a review:

- Whirlpool had originally and unwittingly sailed into a Point of Decision without fully engaging its high core values.
- The first unseen result? *A drop in integrity*. Proof: denial.
- The second, related but visible result: *A drop in revenues and profits*.
- The third, institutional result: *A loss of teamwork*. Proof: fear.
- The fourth, retrograding result: *Feral survivalism*. Proof: hiding, blaming, and lying.

This is the classic countdown to self-destruction using the Enron, Arthur Andersen, WorldCom, Bethlehem Steel corporate suicide playbook.

Fortunately, Whirlpool had senior people at the table who were willing to accept, state, and stand for brutal, principled candor. Mike Thieneman had to feel a jolt of fear in the North Board Room, just as Chris Kay had experienced when Will Sampson threatened him.

But both execs knew that facing momentary emotional discomfort was a small price to purchase institutional integrity.

The truth was that in the last year, courageous leadership had not universally occupied the Whirlpool field. It had been degraded by moments and movements of individual self-interest. The consequences—profit losses, missed targets, loss of teamwork, hiding, blaming, and Darwinian mud wrestling—then became predictable.

Now Whirlpool got it: it had to listen, respond, and lead more effectively. To do that, Whitwam challenged his top executives to define their true high core values, their authentic operating principles. In the following weeks, he brought them together.

"What are our values?" he asked. He asked them to clarify their answers. "Meaning what?"

He hosted "values challenge meetings," which resulted in a new set of high core values.

The company had been tested in a Point of Decision. It began when senior people lacked the guts to hear and accept negative data. Then lost revenues triggered another retreat from principled executive behavior. Instead of facing the truth and accepting responsibility, individual execs tried to hide and blame and lie.

The company righted itself by seeing that its high values were in crisis. It demonstrated courage by accepting that central truth.

It showed courage by demanding a true redefinition of, and recommitment to, high core values. It then intentionally leveraged those now-accepted values to elevate executives who lived them and to change-out execs that did not.

It was March 2005 when Mike Thieneman, in a gray wool turtleneck, looked out his window at a wintry Lake Michigan.

"Let me tell you the real story," he said. "The real win wasn't that we salvaged our losses the next year. It wasn't that we had the guts to later order an expensive product recall."

He smiled. "The real win was that Dave took action to do something with the company about its values."

He faced me. "That's what equipped us to negotiate our corporate inflection points, what you call the Points of Decision."

Mike Thieneman smiled from the eyes as if it were spring in the Rockies, as if he could see past his midwestern production plants and Italian sales forces and Brazilian engineers to see visions and to dream dreams. "Do you see what it did?" asked Mike. "It let us have shining eyes. Shining eyes see possibilities. Possibilities produce hope. This remains a company worth working for."

That's because self-concern only powers the short sprints, while high principles inspire our best efforts and empower us to robustly and courageously run the interesting paths set before us.

# Part Two

# COURAGE IN ACTION

We've seen the power of courage. We've also been reminded of the dangers of cowardice and apathy.

When an executive shows courage by facing personal fears, even his or her critics are secretly inspired. But when a boss folds to uncertainty, the courage and capability of the organization become as useful as confetti in a tornado.

Courage is a stunning quality: it is learnable. I, a former poster boy for cowardice, know this. In an inner-city ghetto, I accepted fear as my master and made daily sacrifices to it from a quaking heart. Bullies cultivated a taste for my blood. Tiny tots and girls fed up by my crying could pound me. My two exceptionally clever moves of fleeing and blaming others proved unsuccessful. I shouldn't brag, but I was a very entertaining little kid.

I was sent to a YMCA boxing program to save my life. The tank top kept falling off because it required shoulders. In shorts, black socks, and scuffed Buster Browns, I looked like a toothpick in a tutu.

My coach recoiled. "Aw, cripe, kid, ya make me wanna cry." Facing a body bag that was bigger than me, I burst into tears. When

Coach hit the bell for me to fight, I dived through the ropes, instantly smacking into a wall that my acute myopia had failed to detect.

Coach Tony knew that training and practice reverse the habits of fear. It is the one way that courage is learned.

With his intervention, I watched. I learned. I tried. I improved. Because the coaches were intentional and time is kind, I became an assistant boxing instructor, teaching younger lads the science of self-defense. I'm not as active in boxing as I once was, but my understanding of the power of courage has grown even more steadfast.

A boxing ring can symbolize for us the ability to overcome fear and to learn courage. Today's fast-paced corporate ropes are our learning labs, our modern gymnasia in which we can develop and practice the specific skills that constitute the competence of courageous living.

Instead of facing right crosses, left hooks, kidney punches, and jabs out of a clinch, we face people who withhold, cut corners, gossip, feud, exaggerate, blame others, steal credit, and spread angry criticism, stress, and dismay. The business ring can be even more dangerous to your health.

In Part Two, I can serve as your coach. Courage is relational. Learning courage requires a relationship with a coach, a teacher, a mentor. In the chapters and stories that follow, you will learn the ropes of principled conduct and courage.

Courage is a deep-seated, fundamental human competence that leverages our other abilities. It invokes within us our absolute best selves.

The tremendous results purchased by courageous behaviors can't be replaced.

Let's put on our gloves.

# 6

# COURAGEOUS COMMUNICATION

> You cannot continuously improve interdependent
> systems and processes until you progressively perfect
> interdependent, interpersonal relationships.
> —*Stephen R. Covey*

A coach once said to me that Bill Conti's great *Rocky* theme was so stirring that it could get Chicken Little to climb into the ring.

If, after hearing that soundtrack, you felt inspired to learn to box, I'd teach you how to stand. I'd show you how and where to plant your feet so you could align your head, your back, and your center of gravity with the ability to take quick action, to advance, and to defend. Then I'd show you hand and glove positions.

In similar fashion, if you're tired of office friction, a lack of candor, a failure of teamwork, toxic disputes, and pointless conflicts, you are probably more than ready to learn courageous communication.

I'm about to show you how to center your backbone on the power of courage and to plant your feet squarely on principled relations.

In boxing, if you cross your feet, you can end up snorting aromatic spirits of ammonia while gazing at bright ceiling lights.

In life, you get exactly the same outcome if you cross up your relationships.

In courageous communication, principled behavior produces incomparable dividends. As you practice, you become better and results improve until you become masterful in leadership and in problem solving.

## The Case of TPMG

When ethical and economic HMO failures were in season, Kaiser Permanente emerged ethically unscathed. Nonetheless, it experienced historic financial reverses that marked a troubled U.S. health industry.

In 1997, Dr. Robbie Pearl, CEO of The Kaiser Permanente Medical Group (TPMG) of Northern California, faced a Point of Decision.

He knew that doing business as usual in the face of change and severe competition could be disastrous. But how would his five thousand M.D.'s, thirteen thousand nurses, fifty-four thousand employees, and three million members avoid crisis? Where to place the mass of institutional focus and resources?

We know that major institutional upgrades, such as relationship-centered patient care, require intentional advocacy by senior leadership.

Terry Stein, M.D., and Bob Tull, Ph.D., the chief architects of the task, invited me to brainstorm with them. They taught me to focus on behaviors as the index of change and to emphasize empathy consistent with extensive research into patient priorities.[1] The result of their expertise was Leadership Communication for Chiefs, the program in which I met Dr. Fred Baring and six hundred of his fellow chiefs.[2]

Each of TPMG's chiefs of service was a player-coach—a top physician who also had to manage a major, complex department. It's like being a school principal while teaching classes, settling schoolyard disputes, coaching two sports teams, and answering to the superintendent, the school board, and parents while hiring, firing, running summer school, and selling popcorn at basketball games.

But as a group, the chiefs didn't practice courageous communication. This is no reflection on them; it's a statement about American institutions going back, perhaps, to the image of the silently suffering, tooth-grinding, emotionless cowboy who only answers to his horse.

When I met Dr. Baring in 1998, he demonstrated the behaviors of avoidant communication that were common not only in the health industry, but also in law, theology, business, accounting, higher education, professional sports, government, nonprofits, and any other organization that included human beings. These behaviors had become unattractive spikes in TPMG patient satisfaction surveys.

In college, Fred Baring had been the class genius, master of sarcasm, maven of social domination, and a three-sport letterman. He had become the brilliant Dr. Baring—a Schweitzer of his clinic and Typhoid Mary with his staff. He, like many of us, listened poorly, was quickly critical, was often negative, was occasionally intimidating, yet failed to face conflicts directly. Even though Kaiser physicians aren't encumbered with the burdens of private practice, Baring increasingly disliked his commute, his staff, his unending feuds, and his profession. I sensed the negative impact on his family, particularly in his relationship with his teenage daughter.

As part of the TPMG education that would transform leadership, communication, and relationships, Baring and other chiefs of service were asked to name their top communication challenges. Here's what they listed:

- Solving personality and group conflicts
- Talking to angry, uncommunicative staff or people
- Coaching underperformers and average performers
- Giving required performance feedback

Chris Kay and Mike Thieneman—two unusually gifted senior executives—would recognize these issues on their major personal challenges list.

We asked the participants, "What keeps you from jumping into these four issues and just resolving them?"

Some chiefs looked at each other with rueful grins. Others looked down. Some crossed their legs. Others stretched.

When they began to speak, here are the reasons they gave:

"I want to avoid negative emotions."

"I don't want disapproval or to become part of the conflict."

"I don't want to cause any harm."

"I don't want to look bad."

"I don't want to make matters worse."

"I don't want to fail."

"I don't want to be demoted or lose my job."

Let's reflect for a moment on this amazing list. It expresses the fears that flow in almost every executive's—and every other human's—River of Fear. They're on my list, and I expect that they're on yours.

"What do these factors share in common?" I asked. Silence.

"That's very interesting," a chief finally piped up. "It's all about fear."

"Any disagreement with that assessment?" There was none.

"So what's the cost of answering our fears?" I asked.

"Fear keeps us from solving problems," said one.

Another voice said, "Problems we're expected to solve."

I nodded. "That's a lot of power to give to fear. I want you to imagine I'm your cowardly boss. I come to you and say, very clearly, 'Under no circumstances are you to solve any tough problems in your department. Don't ruffle any feathers. If someone does a wrong thing, just ignore it. Don't make waves, and it'll go away. Under no circumstances are you to make a principled stand. If you see abuse, go with it.'"

"Now," I said, "how do you feel?"

"I'd like it," said a chief. "It takes the load off my shoulders. Two seconds later, I'd hate it. There's no way I could follow that order."

"But," said another, "we let fear stop us." This was a short, gray-haired woman with enormous presence. Her lips flattened into a single line as she exhaled through her nose. "We just told ourselves that we're supposed to solve these problems, but we're afraid to."

"Thank you," I said. "Anyone disagree with that assessment?"

Most shook their heads. No one disagreed.

"We're talking about fear. Fear can paralyze our good intentions. It stops us from communicating effectively. We let it dominate our courage. Let's shift gears and look at it when it's used *in* communication: How good is fear as a motivator?"

"It works!" said Fred Baring. Light, almost nervous laughter.

"Yes. But it creates resentment and pushback," said another.

"I agree with that last comment. Fear's a terrible way to influence people," said a chief.

"But you have to admit that it gets results," said another.

"Yes. Bare minimums in performance. And it drives turnover."

As the discussion continued, these medical chiefs, who have unusual professional authority in American society, concluded forcefully that fear was a poor motivator. Contrary to popular belief, fear was an inefficient motivator, even in the short run.

But fear's greatest threat? It stopped chiefs from resolving thorny problems. This in turn diminished the quality of care, compromised values, and threatened professionalism, teamwork, and profitability.

As courageous communicators, they called for a prescription in communication that would not allow fear to stop them from creating consistently principled relationships. They, like all of us, wanted an alternative to silently and passively living with the high costs of anxiety and hesitancy.

TPMG, facing its Point of Decision, had committed to teaching leadership and courageous communication to its department chiefs. They, in turn, would be expected to lead their people to enact principled relationships with their staffs and three million patients.

## Raising the Bar

The State Bar of California, a semigovernmental agency, was spending $30 million a year on lawyer misconduct. This was but a fraction of legal malpractice costs, which were estimated in excess of $1 billion a year.[3] Citizens looked at lawyers as not being much better than drug lords.[4] The state's lawyer jokes outnumbered lobbyists in Congress. I winced when the State Bar, managing the largest body of professionals in the world (140,000), responded with an image campaign. I winced again when I was appointed the State Bar's senior executive for legal education and supported the imposition of mandatory education on our lawyers to address attorney error.

But what to teach? We were at our Point of Decision.

A brilliant Bar executive, Karen Betzner, led a comprehensive survey to learn what clients wanted of their lawyers. The answers were as follows:

An open, communicative, committed relationship

An honest, candid, and principled relationship

A competent attorney

A fair fee[5]

This was a replay of the TPMG survey of patients. No clamor for results—instead, a crying need for communication and relationship.

That's a target for life and a strategic goal for business.

We need encouragement to live well. Early motivation research by Frederick Herzberg at the University of Pittsburgh remains valid: higher-order needs (achievement, recognition, the work itself, responsibility, and advancement) define job satisfaction and the willingness to continue work more than pay and benefits do.[6] The Minneapolis Gas Company's twenty-year longitudinal study of forty-four thousand employees showed that advancement, type of work, and pride in the company outweighed salary and benefits.[7]

Yet these uncontroversial findings about the *how* of corporate success are not nationally accepted. I went to school with a gifted person who was world-class brilliant, NCAA-level athletic, dazzlingly charismatic, and movie-star handsome—in other words, my exact opposite. I was from tough streets in which violence was customary, but I was shocked by his gross disrespect for women. This individual rose to an exceptionally high position as the number two

85 percent of organizational success depends on communication and interpersonal skills.

80 percent of our waking hours are spent in some form of communication.

75 percent of supervisory, sales, and support staff hours are communication-related.

70 percent of all organizational errors are attributable to poor communication and listening.

We recall only 17 percent of what is said to us, but we remember 80 percent of the emotional message.[8]

person for ethics in one of the federal government's largest departments. In 1999, he was found guilty of forcing sexual liaisons upon the wives of his division executives. He had told them that if they didn't submit to his demands, he would ruin their husbands' federal careers.

In contrast, my law school mentor was also brilliant but quiet and unassuming. Often rumpled, delightfully wry, and physically unimposing, Edgar Bodenheimer had been a Holocaust refugee and a Nuremberg prosecutor whose teachings about the sanctity of high law yet ring in King Hall. When he passed away in 1991, many mourned. I still miss him. I will always treasure what he taught me about jurisprudence, natural law, and relationalism. In natural law, he said, there are aspects of human behavior that are universally admired and aspects that are universally abhorred.

Professor Bodenheimer taught me about enduring principles in the practice of law for the benefit of the weak and in the interests of justice.

My schoolmate, the ethics officer, had on other occasions demonstrated admirable physical courage in combat. But he lacked moral courage in life. This was obvious in his unprincipled communication.

It became patently obvious in his relationships with those with less power—the litmus test for our character. He ended an apparently brilliant career in shame and disgrace.

My law school mentor was a person of integrity and courage. He lived humbly but well, courageously improving the lives of others, surrounded by love and honored by all who knew him.

When we plant our feet firmly in courageous relations and measure our stance in the strict ethics of our relationships, we are in position to multiply results instead of flailing in high-friction stress as a victim of our own unresolved needs.

## Relationships, Resources, and Results

Dr. Robert R. Blake, pioneering behavioral scientist and inventor of the Managerial Grid, said that results are resources passed through relationships.[9] But most corporate relationships are hamstrung by an unhealthy level of individuality and competition. This bleeds off about two-thirds of the original resources committed, which in turn substantially reduces results.

Seldom can we increase resources. But improving relationships produces a one-to-one upswing in results.

Good Relationships + Resources = Results

There's something inappropriate in reducing relationships to a mathematical formula. But if we were to do it, this concept would look like this:

$$CR_1 + R_2 = R_3$$

Yehia Maaty, director of general market operations for Xerox Egypt, looked at this equation in 2004.

"OK, Gus, yes, I agree: courage transforms organizations. But this is not a transformative equation. It is simply a routine equation."

I'd been using my adaptation of Blake's formula for more than a decade. I stopped my defensiveness and said, "Please tell me more."

"I agree with you that courage changes everything. But courage isn't *additive*. It's *multiplicative*. It's synergistic."

He was right; U.S. profitability studies such as *Built to Last*, *Good to Great*, *Contented Cows*, and *A Great Place to Work* reveal the universal transformative effect of principles and principled relationships on profitability, sustainability, and longevity.[10]

Jim Collins's eleven original *Good to Great* firms outearned the general market by nearly seven times for over fifteen years.[11]

By contrast, not only did their rivals fall behind; most of them failed to survive as independent entities.

Failing to be principled doesn't mean second place; it invites an institutional crossing of another, more fatal river.

What's the link between *Good to Great* research and courageous communication? The great firms had CEOs with the character to subordinate their egos and lead with humility. Humility invites principled relationships as certainly as arrogance cripples them.

These courageous CEOs quickly and decisively dispatched people who lacked character or who damaged principled relationships. This sustained corporate morale, unified firms around values, and drew the strongest leaders. They lived and communicated an ambition for the company and its employees instead of for the self.

My engineering profs could craft a formula for this truth. It would describe how standard corporate relationships *impede* results by two-thirds while courageous relationships multiply profits by a factor of seven.

This gives the new courage algorithm:

(Courageous Relationships) × (Resources) = 7 × (Results)

Or mathematically:

$$(CR_1)\,(R_2) = 7(R_3)$$

Ethically courageous relationships *multiply* results by a factor of 7.

Transformational synergy—historical leveraging of limited resources—results when relationships are courage-based $(CR_1)$.

Leadership creates synergy. Synergy is multiplicative. This trumps subtractive arithmetic in which avoidant and hesitant communication hamstrings relationships and results.

Let's return now to the story of Kaiser Permanente and look more closely at the Courageous Communication Model that emerged from that program.

# 7

# THE COURAGEOUS COMMUNICATION MODEL

Courage is what it takes to stand up and speak;
courage is also what it takes to sit down and listen.
—*Winston Churchill*

As the Kaiser M.D.'s took a coffee break at the Chaminade Conference Center in Santa Cruz, California, I noticed Dr. Baring holding forth. He was complaining that work was suffering because of "flavor-of-the-month communication training."

Communication's overrated, he was saying. "What more do we need to know?" Returning from the break, we divided into small groups to practice the communication model that we had learned earlier that morning. We sat in soft chairs. Warm coastal sunlight spilled inward as clouds scudded toward Asia.

Dr. Baring waved off the four challenges that the chiefs had earlier identified as their toughest: conflicts, difficult employees, low performers, and performance feedback. He said that he needed no help.

I pictured a tough bandoleered Sierra Madre bandit with a gun saying, "Communication? We don't need no stinkin' communication!"

"But how *successful* are you, Fred?" asked a female chief.

Baring said, "Like a pig on skates. But I don't have any fear."

"Give me an example," I said, grinning, "of a talk that failed."

"I have so many. OK, how about Quince, Dr. Quincy. This man is always late to clinic. It got so bad that I had to tell him that I'd dock his pay."

"How'd Quince react?" I asked.

"He got real red in the face, turned his back, and walked away."

"Did Quince start coming in on time after your talk with him?"

"Heck, no," said Fred. "But I docked him, quick and hard."

Some of the other physicians seemed to know Fred Baring's aggressive reputation. I felt silent judgment as Fred twisted in his chair.

"We all experience this, don't we?" I asked. "More examples?"

One doctor offered a similar story. It had the same outcome: no changed behaviors despite repeated counseling and penalties. Lots of words, too much time, ample worry, plenty of frustration, and no results. It seemed that no one wanted to go through the pain of correcting a valuable clinician for minor faults like rudeness, lateness, poor charting, anger, impatience, poor patient skills, or the inability to create a team or to encourage others, even though the cumulative effect of these failures was expensive in teamwork and outcomes.

"Could our communication model work for these situations?"

Fred Baring shook his head. "No. I don't believe in mollycoddling."

"Good. I don't either. Help me out. Define 'mollycoddling.'"

"It's tolerating B.S. It's putting up with substandard performance."

"Dr. Baring, I'm with you. No mollycoddling here. The purpose of the model is courageous communication." I smiled. "No chickens allowed!"

He nodded.

## Dr. Baring Tries to Solve a Performance Problem

I say, "Would you show us what it's like to work with Dr. Quincy?" Dr. Baring agrees to act out his talk with the tardy Quince.

A group member offers to play Quince. Fred says, "You know the actor Wilfred Brimley? That's what Quince's like." He gives examples.

Two chairs face each other in the bull ring; the two men sit and face each other as if they were alone in the clinic.

Dr. Baring is stern. He seems larger. He is a big personal force, with what some Chinese call *ti-mien*, sucking up gravity and air. He leans in, showing some teeth, unhappy, and says, "I need you here on time."

"Sorry, Fred," says the chief playing Dr. Quincy, leaning back. "I got a new car. Doggone if it didn't break down this morning."

"With you, it's always something. Bad traffic. Highway accidents. Or a toaster blows up." Baring throws a hand with "blows up."

"Bad luck, I figure," says Quince, automatically crossing his legs.

"Darn it, Quince, I need you here on time." Hand-chop gesture.

Quince replies slowly, "You know, I've been doctoring a long time. Been thinking about retirement. Maybe it's time. Think I should retire, Fred?"

"Come on! Not that! Jeez! I need you to cover your shifts." Fred hears his own anger, puts his hands up, sighs, and leans back.

"Good point." Quince checks the time. "Patients in two minutes."

Fred tries two more tacks, his voice louder, his gestures more animated. He's working harder—a big and true effort—but without success. His sincerity—and his frustration—are genuine.

Now, we all remember why we don't do this kind of talk. It's as if the list of fears has jumped from the flipchart to land in the room: Fear of conflict. Fear of not looking good. Fear of making things worse.

I thank them both, and we applaud their realism. Fred Baring admits that the doc playing Quince did a good job; it's Quince's way.

## The Courageous Communication Model

Perhaps Fred Baring was right: communication may be overrated. No big deal: without good communication, relationships become combative and self-centered, results implode, departments fail, people are fired, marriages end, children crash, companies dive, people die of loneliness, and nations collapse.

Dr. Baring will fail as a leader, and TPMG's leadership initiative will lose credibility if this brilliant, gifted, and high-profile chief can't competently communicate with his troubled department.

So what's different about the model you're about to learn? How does it differ from assertiveness training, echo-back, broken record, and other communication techniques?

It's the difference between leadership—courageously inspiring people to their best selves—and management—allocating resources with precision and care. It's the difference between crossing the river to genuinely solve problems and being stuck on the wrong bank of the River of Fear.

*Assertiveness training* aims at better expression of the self. It is mostly about generating respect for an often passive speaker. It results in an important outcome: the increased dignity of the individual.

The objective of *courageous communication*, as we saw in Chapter Six, is to produce principled and collegial relationships. Its goal is to live rightly. This goes beyond a few thoughtful communication techniques designed to advance an individual's right to speak up. Courageous communication produces key intentional outcomes—ethical collegiality, effective teamwork, unified operations, and sustained productivity—the dignity of *all* persons.

Assertiveness training can operate successfully in a low-values or even a values-free setting.

Courageous communication reflects high core values because it is based on integrity. It creates values-centered results and a values-centered corporate culture and directly challenges a low-values environment.

Let's look at the four steps of the Courageous Communication Model.

1. **C**ommunicate collegially.
2. **L**isten actively with **E**mpathy.
3. **A**sk questions on point.
4. **R**elate respectfully.

As a mnemonic device, note that the italicized letters form the acronym CLEAR.

"What's the best way for us to learn the model?"

"*See it, do it, teach it,*" said a chief.[1]

"Thank you—that's it, exactly! You saw me demonstrate the model in class. Who'd like to try it now?"

They agree. Dr. Rachel Smith asks if she can be the first.[2]

"Please!" says Fred Baring, instantly fleeing the hot seat. Others laugh. Fred smiles, welcoming Dr. Smith with a bow and a gallant sweep of his arm.

## Trying Out the Courageous Communication Model

Dr. Smith sits, squarely facing the doc who is playing Dr. Quincy. Smiling disarmingly, she offers her hand. Quince reluctantly shakes. Even though he projects a sharp and angular resentment, Dr. Smith's body language courageously conveys openness, fairness, caring, and candor.

---

1. Communicate Collegially

   Approach others with unconditional positive respect. Be ethical, supportive, and encouraging.

---

"Quince, good to see you. How are you doing?" *Show intent to be collegial.* Rachel is placing principle above time pressure and respect above her frustration. Her attitude is encouraging and supportive.

"Fine, thanks," says Quince. He's guarded, waiting for an attack. His energy is flowing into self-defense, not problem solving.

She says, "Thank you again for assessing the patient satisfaction scores. You were a big help. And thank you for giving me these ten minutes." *A warm acknowledgment, rich with encouragement. Rachel showed intentionality by asking for a meeting. No accidental, "oh, by the way" hallway chat for this topic.*

She doesn't treat him as an afterthought; *he is her colleague and teammate.*

"You're welcome." He's still waiting for the other shoe to drop.

---

2. *Listen Actively with* Empathy
   Capture what the other person is feeling—the *in*-feeling—
   in that person's context, without being detached from or
   swamped by it.[3] You must genuinely hear the other person
   and reflect back what you hear.

---

"Doctor, don't waste our time. You're after something."

Rachel hears the words and feels the heat of his emotions. She feels threatened. This triggers the impulse to defend and to argue. Instead, she follows the model by listening actively with empathy. *What's he feeling?* With that, she reflects back.

"You think I'm wasting time and I'm after something. And that's not making you feel very good."

Rachel has captured his position so well that Quince hesitates. But he's intent on not being talked into change and so returns to the offensive.

"Now you're being clever. You're saying things to buy concessions."

Rachel is now a *spellbound listener*—relying on an ability that has irresistible power. Instead of responding with anger, she listens with strength, recognizing that he's suspicious. Again, she reflects back.

"You think I'm being clever and I thanked you so I could get something from you."

"Well, isn't it that true?" he asks hotly.

"I can see you're angry with me, Quince. But I thanked you because you mean a lot to me. Because I need your help." After demonstrating unconditional positive respect and courage by twice reflecting back, Rachel can now attempt to enter into fuller dialogue with him.

Consider her entire manner: a respectful posture, attentiveness, strong eye contact, warmth, positive bearing. These communicate the essence of this exchange: that as a leader and colleague, she respects Dr. Quincy and honors him.

Nothing—not his anger, judgment, or suspicion—can shake her principled resolve to respect him and to act in accord with high core values for the good of the department.

---

3. Ask Questions on Point

   Ask open-ended questions.

---

"Quince, may I ask you something? How do you assess your clinic punctuality?"

There! She asked the *question on point*. She opened with respect, reflected back, and then raised the issue.

This respect-based *asking* is a hundredfold better than the usual *statement* approach, which assumes the guise of an angry parent or drill sergeant:

"You're late! You'd better start showing up on time."

"Is there something wrong with your watch? Or with your head?"

"Do you have any idea of what kind of trouble you cause me and others by being late?"

Quince shrugs. "I guess better than some. Worse than others."

She nods. "That's true. Some are early; others aren't." Again she reflects back his answer, both to capture his emotions and to make sure she understands. If she had misstated his meaning, she'd be able to tell by his reactions. She also reflects back to clearly show that their long-term collegial relationship is more important to the department and the organization than his transient lateness.

Empathy trumps argument. She's building a collegial and courageous $CR_1$.

"I see," he says. "No more Dr. Nice, huh? Now you're on me about being *late*." He challenges her approach to his behaviors.

Even though she's tempted, Rachel doesn't deny his feelings or respond defensively. *More anger. He's afraid of something. Maybe he's afraid of having to change. Reflect back.*

She smiles. "Quince, I can see that you think I'm out to get you. But Dr. Quincy, what I want is to understand what's happening." Positively, firmly, she says, "I want to understand your viewpoint on timeliness." Rachel needs CR,, and she wants to understand why a smart professional like Quince is late. Until then, she can't help solve the problem.

He takes a breath, reloading. "Want *my* viewpoint? My viewpoint, Dr. Smith, is that sometimes we work overtime and *sometimes we get here later than others,* OK?" He's raised his voice to scare her off the topic, to ease his emotional discomfort, to keep her from hitting home on his personal faults.

She nods, smiling. "I agree." This is a huge statement, for it's here, when the other person shows negative emotion, that we normally fold our tents and give up by getting angry, getting even, or getting lost.

"Quince," she says, feeling the flow of energy and using some of that in her voice, "what's the impact when you're on time?"

*Do you see this?* She doesn't argue. Instead, she invites his thinking. She knows it's *Quince's* issue, and she wants him to do the math, to work the problem instead of lighting her own hair on fire and jumping into his bad feelings like a moth diving into a lantern.

By asking questions, she can invite his taking responsibility. This is far better than swinging away again and again when there's no pitch over the plate. This is better than striking out and leaving a failed talk with Quince's punctuality monkey still pinned securely to her back. She doesn't want to end up like Fred Baring, using a louder voice and harder gestures only to fan at the plate, become officially ineffective, and resolve to never try again while still being plagued by a direct report's lack of punctuality.

She asked the question on point. Now she can weather the storm.

He says, "When I'm on time? Nothing. It's all hunky-dory."

"That's right! We cut wait times. Cut stress. Give better care."

"But that's not what you're talking about, Dr. Smith." Quince's arguing. If Rachel argues back and gets mad, she'll have abandoned her high core values and her $CR_1$ commitment with a colleague. Deep down, Quince knows this: *Then he can come in late again.*

Rachel remains in the ring; courageously, she keeps to the model.

"You seem to doubt my position," she says.

"I am not!" His frustration is clear. Later, he'll tell the group that Rachel Smith's courageous respect made it difficult for him to continue to fight her and he was ready to agree with her but felt he should remain hostile for the exercise.

Meanwhile, Rachel remains calm and intentional. Undeterred by negative feelings, she collegially leans forward, as if she were talking to a trusted comrade who respects her. The other members of the group will later say that they felt enormous admiration for her.

"I want *your* focus. Quince, I need your help in this. It's important to me." She's respected him by listening, raised the key issue with a question, and empathetically asked his help by recognizing his feelings. She's emphasizing his importance to her—not to the unit, to costs, to profits, or even to patients. To *her. That's $CR_1$.*

She hasn't used authority; she's used a principled approach.

She doesn't belittle him about his fault; she's supportive.

She doesn't avoid the issue; she encourages him to solve it.

Her anger and judgment of Dr. Quincy would have nullified her attempt to fix a problem. Her courage, on the other hand, strengthened her resolve to respectfully challenge a wrong behavior and allowed Dr. Quincy to own the issue.

"I know what this is about," he says. "It's about fining me."

She smiles, which disarms the tension. "It's about *needing* you. Needing your brains. Needing your *help.*"

Rachel doesn't reflect back his statement here because they're sufficiently engaged to no longer require this tool.

She respectfully refuted his statement because she's not interested in fining him or becoming punitive.

"Rachel, I'm not that good at punctuality. Never have been."

*Breakthrough!* Even though this is an exercise, her heart actually lifts. *Now there's an authentic $CR_1$ connection!*

Courageous communication led him to finally own the issue and to recognize the monkey that's had his name emblazoned on its forehead and stamped in bronze on its little propeller beanie.

Even if it's momentary, this is huge. Rachel wants to support Quince's honesty and boldness; warmly, she nods.

But she doesn't rush in. She supports him and his statement and says, "I hate weekend call. Cuts into our kids' soccer games. I get all bitter."

"But you still come in," he adds. "Probably on time."

"I do," she says. "So how do you feel about being late?"

A shrug. "OK."

It's a lie. She nods, not pouncing on his obvious fabrication. Pleasantly, open and patient, Rachel waits. *He was honest before, and if she doesn't press, he'll eventually do it again.*

Silence weighs on him, not on Rachel. She bravely accepts the silence to let truth have its way with him. Now *his* monkey is on *his* back.

"OK," he says, "maybe not that good. It's a problem, I guess."

"Why's that?" Her patience is a model to us all. She's more intent on solving problems relationally than causing more problems with impatience, anger, and judgment, by showing that she's "right." Everyone feels it. Because she's so strong and principled, the battle's going her way. Everyone can see that. Her modeling, even in an exercise, is affecting all of us.

He sighs. "Look, I know when someone's late, it backs up the whole department for the entire day. Causes problems. For many."

Rachel smiles with great empathy and feeling. She is wholly present. With feeling, with sincerity, with strong, clear eye contact, she says, "Quince, you got it. Thank you for saying that." Huge affirmation.

"Look, I guess I could try to leave home earlier. . . ."

*Admission!*

Rachel smiles. Not triumphantly, for the victory isn't over Quince; it's over her own fears. It's a collegial smile, for she's gained an $R_1$ comrade.

> 4. Relate Respectfully
> Focus on support, encouragement, moving forward, partner-
> ing, and accountability.

"That'd be great, Quince. I'm really curious—what stops you now from coming in earlier?" *Now* she can ask a probing question; he's admitted the issue. If she had opened on this, she would have drawn his defensive resentments, a strong, final pushback, a communication defeat, a lingering sour feeling in her gut, and been reluctant to try again.

"I'm distractible; I always see one more thing to do."

Rachel nods. "Happens to me, too."

"How do you avoid it?"

Rachel tells him, in detail.

He surmises that he could do the same.

She asks what he would like to do about that idea.

He'd like to try it.

Rachel asks if he'd be willing to come in five minutes early every day for the rest of the week. On Friday, they could then discuss it. He agrees.

She's communicated collegially; listened actively with empathy; asked questions on point; and related respectfully.

## The Power of Courageous Communication

At first glance, the Courageous Communication Model seems awkward. It's like hitting a tennis ball backhand, tying your shoe, or saying "pencil" in a foreign language, for the first time. But many people play tennis, wear shoes, and speak other languages.

Courageous communication is a learnable skill. We saw its results in Chapter Four, when Chris Kay directly communicated with Will Sampson and Gene Stingley. Coaching, preparation in, and use of the communication model gave Chris the tools to overcome his very natural sense of conflict aversion. He released Will Sampson while keeping Gene Stingley as a valuable colleague, teammate, and contributor. In this chapter, Dr. Rachel Smith demonstrated the learnable behavioral skills necessary for coaching colleagues and others.

Competence comes from practicing a skill until it becomes second nature. Courage in practice is powerful. Practice produces big dividends: fear is faced, which improves important things like decision making. It builds big things like relationships and quality of life.

Courageous communication replaces cowardly avoidance and apathy in relationships. It replaces convoluted arguments, painful paralysis, anxious hesitations, destructive timidity, and fear.

It swaps continuous low-level friction and work dread for values-driven teamwork, productivity, and sustainable results.

And if someone like me, raised well outside American majority culture and innately gifted in nothing, can learn the four steps, it should be easy for you.

The Leadership Communication program was an important element in TPMG's mastery of its Point of Decision. Feedback revealed that the physicians who had received this and other training experienced improved patient satisfaction scores and greater perceived effectiveness.

The corporation enjoyed direct benefits when high core values—courage, integrity, and character (in the form of humility)—were introduced into the results equation and the behavioral skills of courageous communication were learned and added to patient communication skills.

Courage improves relationships as surely as cowardice degrades them. Courage is the lever of leadership, while cowardice invites its collapse. Approaching a Point of Decision, it's crucial to have ample servings of the one and absolutely none of the other.

Three months after the communication training, I met Dr. Baring at his hospital. Although very busy, he appeared to be relaxed and even content. He had learned to enter the ring with a very different set of skills and had been rewarded by greater relational success and departmental efficiencies.

I already knew that he and Dr. Quincy had formed a new and collegial relationship. I knew that Quince was no longer late to clinic. Even more important, Dr. Baring was no longer acting on his considerable anger.

I was interested in how he was doing with another member of his staff with whom he had a challenge and about whom we had devoted a coaching session. But he had someone else on his mind.

"I used your model with my teenage daughter," Baring told me. "It's changed everything."

# 8

## COURAGEOUS FEEDBACK

To sin by silence when they should protest makes cowards out of men.

—*Abraham Lincoln*

Gilbert W. Long of ISEC sits at a conference table in Phoenix, Arizona. He looks at the guy next to him, an executive he's worked side by side with for thirty years, a guy he loves with a go-to-Texas loyalty. But looking at this man, Gil feels like biting a brown snake.

The object of look and loyalty is Don Shaw. Don's wondering why Gil, his closest colleague, is now short-tempered and prone to cursing.

Gil is thick and barrel-chested; Don is tall and lean. Gil was a college All-American quarterback. There's toughness in his square hands, boulderlike head, and no-nonsense voice. Gil is a senior vice-president, a charge-ahead guy and the right-hand exec to ISEC's founding president, the legendary builder Lewis L. Anderson.

Don looks like an angular *pistolero* or a Texas Ranger in *Lonesome Dove,* which happens to be Don and Gil's favorite film. There's a statesman in Don's height and optimism in his voice. The picture of patience, Don is senior executive vice-president and COO of ISEC, a national specialty construction firm. If you've ever spent time at a five-star hotel, a major airport, a science lab, a business building, or a sports stadium, you've seen their work. Don and Gil have spent so much time together they have the same laugh, but lately, Gil's not laughing.

Both get paid to solve problems. They've been stalwart companions, bonded by company loyalty, a love for their people, and a common interest in doing the right thing. Today, the problem is their inability to communicate with each other. It's significant because ISEC is approaching an internal Point of Decision.

The day's agenda: strategic planning. But dark clouds are forming above Gil. Don, who knows details about Gil the way grunts who share foxholes know each other, says nothing.

"What's going on, Gil?" I ask. "Something's chewing on you." I can talk like this because I'm a consultant who's used to being fired.

Gil opens his mouth, the QB ready to call the play. Then he shuts it. Whatever's inside is too hard, too risky. Head shake. "Nothing."

I smile. "A *nothing* like that caused the Hundred Years' War. You guys haven't yet taken the Courageous Communication classes, but Gil, you can let it out here. What you have to say is important."

He says he can handle it. I keep challenging him to say it out loud. He pushes back. Neither of us backs off. Don shifts in his chair. There's enough anxiety for thirty project managers who are two weeks behind in a thunderstorm, and there are only three of us in the room.

"OK," Gil says. "Want to know?" I nod. He takes a deep breath and looks down. "Don," he says sharply, "you're not carrying your damn weight. You haven't for a year. Now you're going to move for personal convenience. That doesn't work for me. It's bull."

Both dislike conflict. Don would rather eat a bushel of horned toads than argue with someone he cares for. Pained, Don admits that the death of his wife and his heart surgery have slowed him down.

Gil says, "Yeah, yeah," and details how Don has missed the pitch, not hit any runners home, and missed suiting up. Don gets defensive. There's no resolution, but something terrific has happened:

What's made these two excellent execs sick is on the table.

Gil glares at me. *See, I let it out, but is it any better? Heck, no!* "You happy now, Gus?" asks Gil, as pleased as a ruptured duck.

"I am. Now we can get to work! I've got a tool for you to use with the info you exchanged.

"It's called Action-e-Reaction. The "e" stands for *emotional*. It's for courageous and real feedback."

## Action-e-Reaction

"What the heck is the point of that?" asks Gil.

"First, you get to talk about the issue. No more denial. No burying it or going around it or just sucking it up. Second, it'll change things because you can communicate better from now on. Third, by acknowledging the real feelings, you're being authentic. That's hard to argue with."

They're listening now because anything's better than feuding.

"Action-e-Reaction has two working parts: the other person's action and the emotional feeling you get from it. Here's an example: when you told Don what was on your mind, I felt good."

He thinks about that. "How does that help me with the issue?"

"My telling you how I feel captures what's happening between us. Your telling Don how you feel is straight-up, dead-on feedback. It's *on point*. That means it's productive data. No more suffering in silence. No more sending mixed signals, of *being* angry but saying you're *not* angry."

"I don't see that. Don knows how I feel." I ask Don if he did.

Don somberly shakes his head. "I didn't know you were angry."

I turn to Gil. "Gil, you just told Don what's going on inside you. That's good. Candor beats a cover-up of feelings, even negative ones, a thousand to one. When we swallow reality and fake being nice, we don't make things better. We make people sick, starting with ourselves.

Dale Carnegie, the original American seer of relationships, said, "When dealing with people, let us remember we are not dealing with creatures of logic. We are dealing with creatures of emotion, creatures bustling with prejudices and motivated by pride and vanity."[1]

"Then it builds up until we think we can't hold it and we lose our temper and attack—we don't make things better either. Leaders solve moral problems, and silence doesn't work.

"This is where Action-e-Reaction comes in.[2]

## We Feel Bad When We're Judged

"If I say to you, 'Gil, you're the south-end of a northbound donkey, and you make the village idiot look smart,' how do you feel?"

"Not good," he says. "Kind of like how I feel now."

"That's right. When someone labels us, we get defensive. Don, how'd you feel when Gil said you were half-stepping?"

"Bad," says Don.

"You bet. We feel bad when we're judged.

"Action-e-Reaction lets us describe what we feel—the emotion—from the other's action. We don't judge the person for the action. Or blame the other for our feeling."

He shrugs. *I hear you talking, but I'm not sure what you mean.*

"Example: a typical negative comment: 'Don, you were a jerk for taking time off for personal issues.' What do you want to say to that?"

"I'd say, 'I didn't do anything wrong,'" says Don. "My wife died and I needed heart surgery. I didn't do that on purpose."

"Absolutely. We defend ourselves. And that goes where?"

"Nowhere," says Gil.

"Exactly."

"So we need a tool that lets us communicate the emotional impact of someone else's action but without judging the person."

## We Can Hear and Accept
## the e-Reaction to Our Behaviors

"Here's an Action-e-Reaction: 'Don, when you took personal time off, I felt like I was left holding the bag.'" I put a loud period at the end. In the silence, the words hit home. I wait, then say "Don, what do you feel like saying to that?"

Don nods. "Interesting. That's completely different. Instead of fighting, I feel like I should apologize. But why is that?"

"When people have the guts to admit how they *feel* about our behavior, we *hear* it. It's genuine. It's courageous. It's about the two of us being real, instead of one of us being a jerk. Even if we don't like it, we get it.

"But when they judge, label, or get angry at us, instantly, we feel defensive. We become defensive. That means an argument."

"Then," said Gil, "how come I still feel like dog puke?"

"How long have you been feeling bad about Don's absences?"

"It's probably been a year. Maybe longer."

"How strong are those feelings?"

"Strong. I've been doing my job and his job. And others'."

"Those strong feelings include being angry at Don?"

Gil nods. "I said so. I feel like I shouldn't. I mean, Sue died."

"How many times did you tell him that you were angry?"

"Never. Not once. Until today."

"Did you tell him that today?"

"Well, in so many words."

"Give him an Action-e-Reaction with the emotional word *angry*."

Gil says, "When you took time off, you made me pretty angry."

I got a small radar blip on that one. Here's why:

When giving feedback on your feelings, we can't *blame* the other person for them. We own our own feelings; they are ours and not his. Reacting to a person's behavior is normal. Although blaming that person for our emotional reactions is also normal, it's not accurate. The courageous person is responsible for his or her own feelings regardless of what others do.

Remember that hiding and blaming are acts of cowardice. We do them because at first they seem easy, not because they're right.

A common mistake is saying, 'You *made me* feel this way' or 'You *made me* angry.' We say this because it's easier to blame than it is to own our reactions to the things that happen. There's a world of difference between saying how you feel in reaction to something and blaming someone for what you feel.

Blaming the other person for your feelings wipes out the benefit of Action-e-Reaction. Instead, state the feeling or emotion you had.

"Gil, try it again without saying he *made you* feel what you felt."

Gil nods and takes a breath. "When you took time off, I felt angry."

"Perfect!" I said. "Action-e-Reaction! Don, say what you want."

Don looked at Gil. "Gil, I'm real sorry I let you down."

"Thank you," said Gil. "It wasn't easy saying this."

"I know I have to buck up," said Don. "And I will."

Gil smiles from El Paso to Galveston. "Thanks, buddy," he says.

Did this exchange sound cold to you? Most of us wouldn't be able to say that we felt let down by a friend who had lost his wife and had been seriously ill himself. Because of camaraderie, we have strong feelings about people at work. Note that because of a *lack* of camaraderie, we also have strong feelings about people at work.

Because of courageous communication—and a Constitution that makes authenticity mortally safe—Americans can leapfrog older cultural traditions and speak genuinely and candidly to each other.

That's how teams are formed. That's how organizational excellence is sustained.

---

When I was courting Diane, she asked me what I was feeling.

I frowned with hard thought. "That a trick question?" I asked.

She smiled. When she smiles, I can hear anything. "Did you know that you have two emotions? One's anger, and the other's hunger."

I thought about that. "OK," I said.

A wonderful laugh. "Gus, you're supposed to have a *lot* of feelings, many emotions. Two's a little on the scarce side."

A list of feelings appears in Exhibit 8.1.

## Exhibit 8.1.  Feeling Words

This is not a comprehensive list.

*Negative Feelings (Too Many of These in the Culture)*

| | | | |
|---|---|---|---|
| abandoned | ambivalent | angry | annoyed |
| anxious | betrayed | bitter | burdened |
| cheated | confused | crushed | defeated |
| despair | diminished | distracted | discontented |
| distraught | dominated | divided | empty |
| envious | exhausted | fatigued | fearful |
| flustered | foolish | frustrated | guilty |
| intimidated | irritated | isolated | jealous |
| left out | lonely | low | mad |
| melancholy | miserable | nervous | overwhelmed |
| pained | persecuted | pressured | rejected |
| remorseful | sad | shocked | skeptical |
| stunned | tense | threatened | tired |
| trapped | troubled | uneasy | unhappy |
| unsettled | vulnerable | weary | worried |

*Positive Feelings (More of These Are Needed in Operations)*

| | | | |
|---|---|---|---|
| adequate | calm | capable | caring |
| challenged | charmed | cheerful | confident |
| content | determined | eager | enhanced |
| energetic | excited | fearless | free |
| fulfilled | generous | glad | gratified |
| happy | helpful | honored | important |
| impressed | inspired | kind | peaceful |
| pleased | proud | recognized | refreshed |
| relaxed | relieved | rewarded | safe |
| satisfied | secure | settled | sure |

Don values Gil. It's not been good for Don to be withdrawn from work and his colleague for well over a year. Nor has it been good for Gil to bottle up the reality of his feelings. Both can support each other and ISEC's success—but only if they're courageous communicators. Action-e-Reaction and the Courageous Communication Model are tools to provide courageous feedback.

To recap, here are the steps to Action-e-Reaction feedback:

1. State the action (the behavior) the other person demonstrated. "When you . . ."

2. Name your emotional reaction to the other person's action. "I felt . . ."

## Confronting an Unprincipled Behavior

Here's another example. Gil was having an ongoing struggle with VP Pete Griggs, a charismatic but difficult executive. "Pete grandstands," Gil said. "He takes credit for what he didn't do."

"Describe one of Pete's specific grandstanding behaviors."

"Donna, in Baltimore, solved a big dustup with X Corporation (a mainstay customer). A huge problem. She handled it. But Griggs took credit."

"What have you done about it?"

"I told him that Donna deserved credit, not him."

"What was the result?"

"He made up a story about how he helped her, which wasn't true. In other words, the result was not a dang thing except he added a new lie."

"How do you feel about that?"

"Not good." He pursed his lips. "Bad. Mostly for Donna."

"Imagine looking Griggs in the eye. No anger. You say, 'Pete, when you took credit for Donna's work, I felt really angry.' Period."

"Pete's not like Don. That won't do any good."

"Will he argue and say you have no right to feeling angry?"

"Maybe not. Tell me again the point of telling him a *feeling?*"

"You're giving him indisputable feedback he can't argue with. You're giving him a result of his action. 'You did this; I felt that.' If instead you accuse him of bad acting and call him names, you'll have—what?"

"An argument that'll go south. What if he says, 'Who cares?'"

"You can say, 'Hey, Pete, thank you for listening,' and mean it."

"That'll do a lot of good!"

"I agree. It will."

"I was being sarcastic."

"And I agreed because it *will* do good. Here's a pointer. To make Action-e-Reaction work, you need a principled relationship, full of encouragement and support. That means you need to catch Pete doing good. *Everyone* needs regular, routine positive feedback. This isn't self-esteem, where you compliment someone for doing little or nothing. This is encouragement, as Kouzes and Posner say, of the heart.[3] Now, for routine positives, you could say, 'Good job. Thanks! Way to go!' For bigger good behaviors, you could say, 'When you did so-and-so, I appreciated you.'"

Gil shook his head. "Pete's hard to compliment. Can't say that."

"You're a leader. With guts. You can say anything that's right."

"You want me to atta-boy a blowhard braggart?"

"When he does good. Even Nero couldn't be bad *all* the time. Courageous communication gets you to the real point. It lets you make it in a way that's heard. That's leadership. It makes possibilities."

"I don't like the idea of complimenting a boaster."

"Man, I don't blame you. But what if it turned out that courageous leaders honor all persons? That they recognize achievement, *particularly* from low performers and braggarts?" I asked Gil about his mentor, his football coach. Did he encourage everyone or just his favorites?

"Yeah, I see it. Coach encouraged everyone."

"That's right. Leaders encourage. It's easy— they are ethical, supportive, and encouraging. They develop others. They don't pull them down, which is what happens with unhealthy competition, gossip, backstabbing, and splitting firms into good guys and bad guys, winners and losers. They don't divide their firms into favorites, friends, and foes."

The Center for Creative Leadership, supported by psychological research data, teaches that tough and challenging feedback can be heard and digested when there are four times as many positive, encouraging, supportive feedback messages as there are challenging ones; in other words, a ratio of 4 positives to 1 negative (4:1).

"This means that faultlessly delivered candid bad news becomes unusable without preceding encouragement. Preceding doesn't mean five minutes before or moments before you deliver the bad news—it means days, weeks, months, and years before.

"Remember? We need principled and courageous (CR$_1$) relationships to get sustained results. Results that are synergistic and transformational.

"It starts with your catching Pete Griggs doing something right.[4] To do this takes courage. It takes courage to go from grinch to greatness."

The next day, Gil held a scheduled meeting in Pete Griggs's office. Gil had checked the list of positive and negative feelings that appears in Exhibit 8.1.

He had found his e-word the way I used to find happy little words with my kids on *Sesame Street*. Today, the one that best expressed Gil's feelings was *disappointed*.

Gil gave him an Action-e-Reaction.

"Pete, when you took credit for Donna's work, I was really disappointed in you."

Pete said, "Like I told you, I helped her with that dust-up."

Gil said, "OK, well, thank you for listening." He stood.

"You being sarcastic?" asked Pete, looking at him closely.

"No. It wasn't easy for me to say that to you. I appreciate your listening to me." Gil got to the door.

Pete stood. "Well, you're, you're welcome."

I asked Gil for the long-term outcome of that Action-e-Reaction.

"I think he'll pause before stealing credit again. I also think that if he pulls another grandstand and I call him on it, he won't do it again."

"What would happen," I asked, "if you provided routine performance returns to Pete and to your other direct reports? Not once a quarter or in the annual merit review, but every week or every two weeks, using the 4:1 positive-to-negatives ratio?"

He considered that, thinking of the time involved.

## The Typical Annual Performance Review

David Shearn has twenty people in a dynamic, high-performance department who want 8:1 feedback from him and no one who gets 4:1.

Right now, he's walking down a hallway, surrounded by people in chairs. He's rubbing his chin. He's a brilliant and thoughtful professional with an air of athletic youthfulness. At this moment, he feels aged. It's time for him to give Joe Sellars his annual performance review.

David knows that he's behind the performance feedback curve. Like a grad student who's not ready for orals, he mumbles, "I should've been giving Joe performance feedback all year. So dumb to have stacked it up until the end."

Down the hall, Joe Sellars keeps looking at the time. David, usually punctual, is late for the performance review. Joe just joined the company fourteen months ago.

"It's pretty clear," Joe says to himself, "that David Shearn doesn't think much of me. David was friendly at first, but the honeymoon's over. Now the guy keeps at a cool distance. Look, I know David's busy, but he couldn't be so busy that he can't take a minute to tell me how I'm doing. Heck, even criticism would be better than not knowing."

David stops outside Joe's door.

"Even before this starts, I know it's going to go badly. Joe's OK, but it's going to be awkward. I'm going to give this guy fourteen months of evaluation in thirty minutes. Most of what I've recorded on Joe is negative, and the sad thing is, he's a good manager."

David Shearn turns to the audience. He and Joe have been role-playing a silent supervisor and a suffering direct report.

"Isn't this true for you?" David, when not acting out dramatic roles in education classes, runs physician education and development for TPMG of Northern California. He is enacting a situation most of us face.

The customary performance evaluations take place annually. This is like changing the oil in a high-r.p.m. NASCAR race vehicle every ten years. Yet many organizations fail to meet this exceptionally low, metal-grinding, people-eating standard in which supervisors don't do their jobs in providing performance feedback, and direct reports, in the resulting silence, actively grow their fears while not improving competencies.

## Routine Performance Returns (RPR)

Everyone needs continual feedback, encouragement, and support. *Continual* is the direct opposite of *annual* or *centennial*. All of us know front-line managers who haven't received their annual review for years.

After David Shearn and Joe Sellars act out their performance review—which is as terrible as David predicted—I ask the audience to describe an ideal situation to replace the horror of the annual merit review. David and Joe listen actively to the suggestions and input of their colleagues. Here's what ensues.

### Quick Incidental Thanks

David's walking down the hall and sees Joe.

"Joe! Great job on that tough case today. The patient was ready to curse, and your courage, your respect, your patience, your professionalism, and your clinical skills saved the day. Thank you so much." (Note the emphasis on high core values.)

"Thanks, David," says Joe.

This dialogue took ten seconds.

### Quick Brainstorming Consultation

We hold up a sign that says TWO DAYS LATER. David knocks on Joe's door.

"Hi, Joe. How are you?"

"Fine. What's up?"

"Got a minute? Great. Remember that difficult case we discussed at staff meeting? How would you handle that?"

"Wow," says Joe. "I'm flattered you're asking." Joe gives his answer.

"Thanks, Joe. You're so good at seeing the upside angle and how it relates back to our high core values."

This dialogue took three minutes.

## Larger Thanks: Action-e-Reaction

Sign: A WEEK LATER. David knocks on Joe's door.

"Hi, Joe. How are you?"

"Fine, thanks. How can I help you?" He looks at his watch. "I'm in between patients. I have time."

"When you told me that you needed more help with the new project to do it right, I was very grateful."

"David, that's great. I appreciated being able to be frank."

This moment of dialogue took twelve seconds.

The audience saw it: clear, core-values thinking plus small dabs of time produce collegiality and $CR_{,}$, a courageously principled relationship.

## Using Questions to Discuss Problems

We use statements to give encouragement and recognition.

In each of the RPR examples, positive feedback was delivered in statement form.

Consistent with the Courageous Communication (CLEAR) Model, we use questions to discuss challenges and problems. This can be summed up with the acronym SEAC, for "state encouragement, ask about challenges."

Instead of saying, "Your performance stank," we can ask, "How do you think that went?" or "How might we have done that differently?" "When we encounter this situation again, how might we approach it differently?" or "What lessons did this experience teach us?"

Asking questions about problems is aligned with respecting, encouraging, supporting, and modeling courage. Anyone can worsen a situation by criticizing and judging; courageous leaders possess the principles to demonstrate disciplined and rightful conduct under emotional pressure.

Sign: THREE DAYS LATER. David knocks on Joe's door.

"Hi, Joe. Thank you for giving me this time."

"Happy to, David. What's up?"

"I've been looking at the Benjamin case. If we see another one like this, as I'm sure we will, how might you do it differently?"

"Did I blow something?" asks Joe.

"We're all learners here. I want to know what we can learn from this file."

"Well, I was so overscheduled that day, I'm not sure what to say."

"Joe, can I share what I saw?"

"Please, David, do that."

David then relates what he observed. "I saw Janelle pull back. I saw Hank shake his head. . . ."

Opening difficult conversations about poor performance or negative emotions is made easier by asking the other person's view instead of delivering an intellectual assessment of the situation.

Asking about troubling issues seems backward, but this is the nature of principled conduct in general. Courage is paradoxical: by doing what seems to represent personal risk, we achieve gains in character. When we engage in the more difficult, principled behavior, we smooth our path for later. When we take the easier, wrong path in the beginning, we end up on broken roads.

## Wrapping Up

The leader's job is to ethically inspire others to be their best selves so that they can act for what is right.

We do this through relational power—by inserting courageous behaviors into intentional relationship building.

Leaders care, listen, relate, and then solve problems.

Routine performance returns are given at the end of observable work. RPR consciously emphasizes high core values, the behaviors of courage, and the positive. This can be provided weekly, as opposed to yearly. It can even be done daily.

When John Gerdelman, chairman of the board of Intelliden and former president of MCI Networks, provides routine feedback, he stresses the positive impact on the organization and his personal gratitude. When Toussaint Streat, my first friend and my first best friend, used to give me feedback to help me become an American lad, he emphasized the positive, even when it was as easy finding a snowball in Tunisia.

Modeling is leadership's ethic, and principled communication is leadership's primary tool. Feedback is communication that reflects respect, support, and courage, and performance feedback is the traffic monitor for excellence. Frequent feedback supports efficient movement to excellence by letting us know how close we are to reaching our highest standards.

Thus performance feedback should be as routine as speech and occur as frequently as people think about how others are doing.

Using the 4:1 ratio of encouraging and positive feedback to challenging feedback, leaders can provide a continuous cycle of fresh and accurate data to keep individuals, teams, and even family members apprised of progress, achievements, kudos, teamwork triumphs, and performance challenges.

Why? Because whatever our jobs or positions, we present ourselves as people of integrity. This makes sense, because all of us know intuitively that a person without integrity is as useful as a blowtorch in a gas station. In fact, that person is a direct threat to everyone's competence and credibility.

Gil and Don have learned to enter the ring of difficult dialogues. They had mastered the delivery of complex and multilayered messages by showing courage and discipline in the approach. By aligning their communication with authenticity, they can then team up in aligning their company with its high core values.

They understand CLEAR—respectful and collegial conversation.

They value the utility of Action-e-Reaction.

They believe in RPR—routine performance returns, with a 4:1 ratio of positive to negative feedback.

These tools are platinum passports across the River of Fear.

Last but not least, Gil and Don had open minds and were willing to practice.

More important, as ISEC approached its Point of Decision in corporate culture, two of its top leaders, by looking at their inner challenges and encouraging each other to be the best they could be, had equipped themselves to lead.

# 9

# COURAGE BY EXAMPLE

Leadership is character and competence. If you can
only have one, opt for character.
—*H. Norman Schwarzkopf*

It's an early autumn morning in 1984. Coffee's brewing, high
achievers are on the road, and U.S. gridlock is gaining steam. A
crimson dawn makes California look like the Far East. I'm walking
Jodie, a fine and loyal Heeler whom we found years before in an
animal shelter.

A child screams. Jodie and I come to alert. Fifty feet away, a
very big man is hitting his son. The kid's under five, his cries pierc-
ing eardrums. I move—then the man says, "I told you *not* to do
that!" I stop. If it were a stranger beating the child, I could intervene. But the father has unwritten law on his side; he can beat his
son, and it's none of my business. Jodie whines, pulling, looking to
me to help the boy. We're powerless. But I feel rotten.

"He's a lot smaller than you!" A woman's voice.

She stands in front of him. Thirty-something, sharp, smart,
physically fit but giving away an easy eighty pounds to a heavy-
weight.

The man stops. He faces her, his blood up, face red, angry at the
boy, mad about life, the petite woman now in the center of his sights.

I know this much: if he attacks *her*, I'll take him down.

But the woman's words have changed us; the man sees himself.
Doubt and then self-consciousness replace his rage. He sees his son
wailing, fighting to escape, a lamb in a trap. Time pauses.

At first, I didn't like the woman speaking out. *It's none of our business.* Then I saw it: a kid was being pummeled in front of me, and I had created a paralyzing reason to not act—to be conflict-averse.

What's worse is that I was the statewide trainer of California's prosecutors. I had a concealed weapons permit, a badge, and a law degree, and I was an officer of the court. The man was a bully, and I had backed down.

Courage trumps authority. It even trumps physical violence.

Luckily, I didn't mutter, "Uh oh! Conflict!" and leave. Fixed by her courage, I brilliantly imitated a fencepost. The man saw me; I seemed to be backing her up. He released his son. Head down, he turned away.

Ironically, weeks later, the San Francisco Family Violence Project asked that I formally institute new and permanent courses in child abuse and domestic violence for the state's four thousand prosecutors. I think they regarded me as a usual suspect of the Closed-Mind Male Tribe, ready to spout the then-familiar refrain, "We can't convict for domestic violence because juries hate those cases." But I remembered a courageous woman standing up to a violent abuser.

Sitting in a capitol conference room, the women of the project and a humbled man designed a new slate of domestic violence training programs that became and remain prosecutorial mainstay courses.

Courage is everywhere. Take an autumn morning at West Point.

## Choose: Courageous Leader or Self-Absorbed Careerist?

"Section, ten-*hut!*" Calls of section leaders echoed down the long corridors of Thayer Hall. Twelve of us came smartly to attention. Our prof entered in step with other instructors in a synchronized academy minuet.

"Sir," said the cadet section leader, presenting arms. "The section is present and accounted for."

Major H. Norman Schwarzkopf, infantry, returned the salute. He was so big that the fall of his hand created a thermal. We were blinded by his bright ribbons and steel decorations, the colors of courage, awards for valor in desperate combat, for mastery of the art of war.

"Take seats," he said precisely. Shakespeare could not have fashioned a more expressive face; the broad-shouldered major with an advanced degree in rocket science displayed amusement, pleasure, anger, suspicion, impatience, disgust. The amusement was for us; the pleasure was for the guys who were trying to learn engineering mechanics; the other emotions, I suspected, were for me.

"You did better than I expected in the WPR." The midterm. "Your reward: I'll teach you the meaning of leadership and courage."

I was as dumb as a pulled stump, but I knew that Major Schwarzkopf was a great man and that if he managed to elude the catastrophes that flank all of us, he'd provide great service for our nation, if not the world. He was the academy's most highly decorated combat veteran of the new controversial war in Vietnam and one of the largest, smartest, and most intimidating human beings I had ever met. I would've listened attentively had he said he was going to teach us how to open a can of pop.

"Imagine that you and the troops for which you are responsible are on an international border. The enemy can cross it and strike at you with impunity. But you can't cross the border. That order comes from the commander in chief.

"Every night, the enemy crosses the border to kill and wound your men, who are Vietnamese Airborne volunteers in your care.

"Every night, you chase the enemy, but they escape at the border, where you stop, *as you are ordered*. Here's the question: when the enemy hits you again tonight, do you pursue them over the line? Or do you follow orders and halt at the border? Questions?" Hands went up.

"If we cross it, will it start a new war?" *No.*

"If we cross the border, can we destroy the enemy?" *Yes.*

"If we cross it and get caught, are we in big trouble?" *Absolutely.
Your president will be very displeased. With you. Personally.*

There were no more questions.

"Gentlemen, STOP or GO? Write."

*It's pretty obvious,* I thought. *If I've learned one thing here, it's that
you follow orders. Especially from the president. Right from wrong. Dis-
obeying the president would be very wrong. OK.* I wrote: STOP.

When the last pencil dropped, Major Schwarzkopf asked, "How
many said STOP?" I raised my hand. So did most of the section.

"How many said GO?" The major smiled at the few hands.

"There are two kinds of people in the world: leaders and careerists. Leaders have character. They act for what is right. They would
die for their men." His words sank into the chalkboards, the walls, us.

"Careerists," he said, making the word sound like a crime against
God, "are self-centered, self-absorbed. They act out of selfishness.
They sacrifice their men for a promotion. They lie to pump up
results.

"They save their skins instead of others'. Careerists can't really
lead because their men do not trust them and will not willingly
follow.

"The correct answer, for a leader, is clear.

"You cross the border. You destroy the enemy to protect your
men. You then take the personal consequences to your career,
knowing that you violated an order but acted for what is right. You
feel pride in getting court-martialed and being reduced to a private.

"Everyone's a leader or isn't. It's not rank. It's *character*."

I grimaced. I had written STOP. I was a natural-born careerist, a
nonleader, thinking first of my tiny career. I was twenty years old,
could march thirty miles with a pack and do fifty pull-ups with
asthma while earning lousy engineering grades. I had full countries
yet to cross to learn the behaviors of courage.

Major Schwarzkopf wasn't teaching abstract theory; only months
before, he had faced that fact pattern on the Cambodian border. A
careerist would've let his men keep dying.

On a summer morning in the Ladrang Valley north of the Chu Pong Mountains and astride an international border, the missile scientist had advised Colonel Ngo Quang Truong and his elite Vietnamese Airborne troops during a successful engagement against the enemy. Ready to be punished for protecting his people years ago in a remote jungle, Norman Schwarzkopf's courage and moral competence marked him then to become our nation's most renowned combat commander.

He had risked his career but had protected his people and therefore his priceless integrity and his authority to lead others.

Our professor had risked everything but principle by demonstrating courage for others.

## Courage Is Everywhere

Diane C. Yu is chief of staff to the president of New York University, chair of the American Bar Association Commission on Women in the Profession, former associate general counsel for Monsanto, one of the top legal minds in America, and a presidential fellow. She argued and won a case before the U.S. Supreme Court and more than thirty cases in the California supreme court. She has the bright eyes of possibility, the grit of a law woman, the presence of a stateswoman, and the ability to order a matchless twelve-course double-happiness banquet in Mandarin. For me, her foremost quality is her ownership of the disciplined behaviors of courage.

When she was serving as general counsel for the State Bar of California, Yu was committed to law remaining a profession that would resist the siren call of business profits. Law would remain a profession committed to ethics, civility, and justice; to the protection of the neediest, in which each and every attorney would be truly worthy of special trust and confidence—and profits would become a consequence instead of a goal.

However, State Bar politics at the time resembled Huey Long's Louisiana lambada as the board of governors engaged in the campaign for the board presidency. Board culture was not, in that season, values-centered, relying instead on vicious competition and flashy showmanship.

Into a board meeting came a fellow senior executive bearing essential advice about the annual legislative bill. This is the bill that authorizes the State Bar to exist. But board candidates for president converted his advice into political cannon fodder. Like Whirlpool in its first reaction to higher costs of materials, the board did not listen to its own troops and began pointing fingers.

Diane Yu watched the board degrade the competence of its highly regarded governmental senior executive. Some members illogically used his wise counsel as a political Frisbee in which the member who could throw it farthest from the table would appear to be the victor.

For another executive to enter a tornadolike criticism of staff would be like testing the sharpness of a buzz saw with your face. I was in that meeting. I felt the need to act but instead measured the likely positive impact if I spoke out. I figured it would be small and could see how my speaking up would merely complicate matters, so I remained silent.

But courage doesn't depend on practical outcomes, risk versus gains analysis, or collateral impact on others—that's *pragmatism*. Pragmatism is the application of practicality, utility, and consequences to decision making.

Courage is addressing wrongs in the face of fear, regardless of consequences, of risk to self, or of potential practical gains. That's why everyone practices pragmatism and risk balancing while so few of us cross the river.

Essential advice was going unheeded, creating immediate economic institutional peril. The future of California's legal profession was on the silent agenda, and good order and discipline were required for that to be rationally considered. That is why Diane Yu stood and spoke, logically detailing how complying with the advice would produce terrific results.

Some board members, given a chance to listen to one of the most powerful, gifted, and collegial advocates in the world, turned on her as if this were a demonstration of sharks in a feeding frenzy. They questioned her judgment and criticized her counsel. Diane Yu could have backed down; she did not. Respectfully and cogently, she fearlessly recited her advice.

The State Bar of California had unwittingly sailed into a Point of Decision without using core values or high operating principles.

The first result? A drop in personal courage and organizational integrity, with a rapid collapse of remaining teamwork.

The second result: the board rejected staff advice, and in short order, the state government defunded the State Bar, exposing it to a battle of political parties. Many senior staff left. In time, the board was required to lay off 80 percent of its staff and shut down most central organizational functions.

The third, institutional result: hiding, blaming, feral survivalism.

It was another classic countdown to self-destruction using the Enron, Arthur Andersen, and WorldCom corporate suicide playbook.

Yu demonstrated the difference between courageous leadership, which is principle-centered, and pragmatism, which is the risk-weighing assessment of probable consequences.

Quite the opposite of committing intellectual or professional suicide, a gutsy stand for principle regardless of risk is the Mosaic, Aristotelian, Confucian, and best use of intelligence, learning, and wisdom.

It has always separated Pericles from Coriolanus, George Washington from Benedict Arnold, and Abraham Lincoln from Warren Harding.

Courageous leadership is about utilizing all of our brains, character, and spirit to advocate principles regardless of the odds, heedless of fear, apart from collateral impact, and independent of personal career needs.

That's exactly what each of us requires as we face our own borders, our personal Rivers of Fear, our family challenges, and our institutional crises.

The stories of high character in this book have inspired me and many others to learn and practice the behaviors of courage.

They have encouraged me to look at leadership through its decisive lens—courage. When we use the lens of courage, the world changes. It's time to apply that vision in learning the three elements of courageous leadership.

# 10

# COURAGEOUS LEADERSHIP

We must become the change we want to see in the world.

—*Mahatma Gandhi*

I promised that after setting the table with courageous communication and before describing courageous problem solving, we'd discuss courageous leadership. Let's explore leadership now.

## Three Types of Motivating Power

Since the time of Og the Caveman, people have had only three ways to get others to act. One of them is the best.

---

The first power is *authority:* do this *or else.*

The second power is *reward:* do this *and I'll give you that.*

The third power is *courage:* ethically modeling and inspiring others to be their best selves and to act courageously for what is right.

---

The abusive father used first-power violence on his small son. Members of the State Bar board of governors demonstrated the first power when they used threats as a response to unwanted legislative advice.

Enron's Andy Fastow abused the first power by using his authority to punish members of the Management Review Committee who opposed his recommendations. He then abused the second power by rewarding those who agreed with him as he used the treasury for personal needs.

In sharp contrast, two leaders we've just considered—H. Norman Schwarzkopf and Diane Yu—boldly modeled the third power by taking risky stands for principle. Instead of speaking to our base survival need, they addressed our better, higher-order selves.

### The First Power: Authority

- Authority or force impels dashes of fear-driven effort
- First: relief, resentment, lower esprit, productivity
- Then, because of a failure to fulfill higher-order needs: paralysis of innovation, lower enthusiasm, reduced work and life longevity

The first-power manager relies on authority, autocracy, and domination. In my experience, charismatic executives who generate blind obedience in others usually default to first-power behaviors. Peter Drucker notes that charisma can undo leaders by inviting their inflexibility and resistance to change.[1]

When this person is under stress, great anger and dire threats can result. This can spawn communication dysfunction, wreck teamwork, destroy individual initiative, and lead to a toxic workplace and work dread.

Normally, we operate on our strengths. When stressed, we do so with even greater energy, But if these actions don't produce desired results, we feel greater stress. In this mode, we show impatience, disrespect, anger, and other failures of emotional management as our worst behaviors surface. We can then end up in the unconscious grip of destructive conduct. Under stress, the first-power manager defaults to even more dramatic expressions of negative emotions, which further separate the manager from desired results.

## The Second Power: Reward

- Money and perks produce dashes of passionate, greed-driven energy
- First: willingness to cut corners, sacrifice values, and inflate results
- Then, because of a failure to fulfill higher-order needs: envy, low spirit, reduced productivity, and turnover as workers continue to seek higher pay

The second-power manager uses increasingly higher monetary rewards, bonuses, perks, and privileges, encouraging greed, envy, and unhealthy competition.

A manager who relies on rewards can expect (1) to lose people to higher-paying firms; (2) to see envy, schisms, and animosities as the staff compete for the highest material rewards; and (3) to suffer a loss of high core values behaviors. When the low core value is greed, offices becomes sties, and the second power is gearing up to consume the firm; studies reveal that firms that directly seek profits instead of excellence tend to fail in realizing either.

## The Third Power: Courage

The third-power leader ethically inspires others to be their best selves so that they can act courageously for what is right. They are personally principled and model courage and humility in making decisions that reflect high core values.

- Courage and integrity result in teamwork, excellence, sustained profits
- First: a passion to fulfill core values and principled team needs
- Then, because of fulfillment of higher-order needs: ($CR_1$) courageous relationships, teamwork, and a core values–based

leadership culture, resulting in sustainable excellence with a deep bench of capable leaders

The third-power leader courageously acts for what is right. This produces enduring success. This option *has* to sound better.

Because the third power has always been the most inspiring and productive method, you would expect a purposeful world movement of courageous executives leading their high core values–aligned departments and organizations to unprecedented, sustainable results.

But because instant self-preservation is our first response, courage becomes the third option. Third-power leaders therefore have great intentionality to be courageous. They cross the river of their own fears while most of us stand idly at the water's edge.

Courageous leaders not only cross the river but also access the first two powers in appropriate ways.

Courageous third-power leaders use the first power (authority) to enforce high core values and operating principles. Using that power, they'll release people when their conduct consistently fails to meet high core value standards. They also use the second power (reward) to provide paychecks, benefits, promotions and bonuses.

But institutional success will depend upon their courage to honor all persons when their guts say to judge and exclude. In the face of fearsome pressure, they will support and encourage low performers; expect principled behavior from each person, especially the technical high performers; and continue to model high core value behaviors. Such leaders intentionally develop the principled behaviors of effective teams.

I began as a second-power leader, trying to motivate with rewards and tolerance of minor underperformance. Staff photos of that time suggest a modest summer camp culture. When I got more authority, like a petty tyrant gaining national control, I used it, trying to influence using the first power (*Cross me and you'll suffer*). I still shudder at those photos of my staff; I am imperious and stern. I look like my father when he was angry. Fortunately, years of instruction and good guidance produced the insight that comes from seeing one's own weaknesses. I've been working on my third-power leadership skills ever since. To test your own leadership style, see Exhibit 10.1.

## Courage, Leadership, and the Third Power

These qualities define the optimally effective leader. The third power is courage. What is *courage*? Take another look at the Character

### Exhibit 10.1.  The Power Assessment Tool

#### What Kind of Leader Are You?

1. Under pressure to produce quick results, I usually
   - a. Quickly give clear and decisive orders
   - b. Offer appropriate rewards for the task and get out of the way
   - c. Ask questions to understand and enroll input and team action

2. When faced with unpleasant news, I usually
   - a. Find where the problem began
   - b. Seek compromises to allow maximum cooperation
   - c. Assume personal responsibility

3. When asked to endorse a questionable decision, I usually
   - a. Support it until I see a more definite reason to object
   - b. Support it in the spirit of mutual support and compromise; whenever I support someone else's initiative, I'm showing teamwork
   - c. Ask on-point questions arising from my doubts

#### Scoring:

The (a) answers tend to describe a first-power manager.

The (b) answers tend to describe a second-power executive.

The (c) answers tend to describe a third-power leader.

Matrix from Chapter Three, bisected by the River of Fear (see Figure 10.1).

Courage defines human and corporate identity. Managers who try to lead without courage are hamstrung before the workforce reaches the parking lot. This is because they won't cross the river to solve the conflicts and frictions that trouble their people and hamper high-end performance and interdependent teamwork. They won't model the courageous behaviors around which their companies can align their conduct. When the tough moral issues arrive, they prefer avoidance.

## Leadership Versus Management: The Final Exam Answer

Why the emphasis on the need for leadership? Why no cries for "more management"? Because we no longer have a "yes, Sir, yes, Ma'am" national culture: individuality has grown faster than credit card debt, learning requires innovation, and success requires character competence.

### Figure 10.1. The Character Matrix

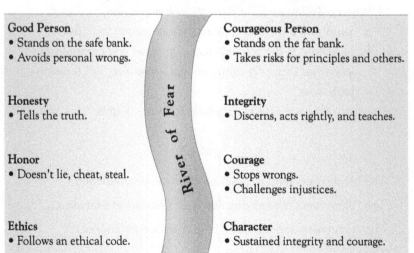

| Good Person<br>• Stands on the safe bank.<br>• Avoids personal wrongs. | | Courageous Person<br>• Stands on the far bank.<br>• Takes risks for principles and others. |
| --- | --- | --- |
| Honesty<br>• Tells the truth. | River of Fear | Integrity<br>• Discerns, acts rightly, and teaches. |
| Honor<br>• Doesn't lie, cheat, steal. | | Courage<br>• Stops wrongs.<br>• Challenges injustices. |
| Ethics<br>• Follows an ethical code. | | Character<br>• Sustained integrity and courage. |

We emphasize the importance of leadership because *people* do more to trigger our crises, bulging waistlines, and thinning hair than *things* do. People rely on vastly diverse values, and these in turn affect the leadership relationships that drive management outcomes.

| *Leadership (People)* | *Management (Things)* |
|---|---|
| Core values | Results |
| Respect | Control |
| Encouragement | Support |
| Empowerment | Organization |
| Recognition | Reward |
| Coaching | Allocating |
| Teamwork | Committee study |
| Feedback | Evaluation |
| Model | Plan |

The Point of Decision for each leader is the ability to master the left-hand skills in order to be able to execute the right-hand functions. Leadership is not management. Leadership is about people and inspiring people. Management is organizations and controlling institutional functions. The effective leader does both by managing courageous and principled relationships.

Consider the reflections on leadership presented in Exhibit 10.2. Of the ten reflections, eight refer to integrity, ethics, responsibility, or character; only two (Lao Tzu and business schools) do not. Notably, however, the latter two focus on the necessary high quality of relationships. One definition (Harvard's) refers to organizations and never mentions people, so technically, in the context of this book, it defines not *leadership* but *management*.

Think of this: if we couldn't define *marketing*, we'd struggle, regardless of innate abilities, with executing it successfully. Not agreeing on what leadership means invites confusion in hiring and developing leaders and measuring their success.

### Exhibit 10.2.  Ten Definitions of Leadership

**Warren Bennis:** Leadership is about character. . . . Managers are people who do things right and leaders are people who do the right thing.[2]

**Stephen Covey:** Managers do things right; leaders do the right thing [paraphrasing Bennis].[3]

**Max De Pree:** The future leader leads through serving . . . [and] has consistent and dependable integrity.[4]

**Peter Drucker:** Leadership is not rank, privileges, titles, or money. It is responsibility.[5]

**Lao Tzu (500s B.C.):** When the best leader's work is done, the people say, "We did it ourselves."[6]

**Norman Schwarzkopf:** Leadership includes two components: competence and character. Ninety-nine percent of the failure in leadership is because of a failure in character rather than competence.[7]

**Sun Tzu (500s B.C.):** If you know the enemy and know yourself, you need not fear the result of a hundred battles.[8]

**Business schools (various):** The ability to motivate or influence others to accomplish organizational goals.[9]

**Harvard Business School:** The ability to ethically move an organization from Point A to Point B.[10]

**West Point:** [Our mission is] to educate, train, and inspire the Corps of Cadets so that each graduate is a commissioned leader of character committed to the values of Duty, Honor, Country.[11]

Let's focus on the traditional business school definition, such as the one I learned many years ago at the University of Maryland: "The ability to motivate or influence others to accomplish organizational goals." This sounds fine, but it is a troublesome definition. Why? Because *motivation* and *influence* are values-free. We can motivate using first (authority and coercion) and second (rewards) powers. We can use lies, manipulation, bribery, duress, threats, physical force, and greed. We can commit ethical missteps and can find ourselves inadvertently following Bernie Ebbers.

## First-Power Authority Is Not Leadership

"What the *!%#$! are you doing!" roared our CEO, Ed Hoss. "Are you trying to make me *puke?*" He was a Ph.D. millionaire with a Cray mainframe between his ears, a yacht in the Chesapeake, and greed growing in his heart. He was brilliant, amusing, dangerous, and irresistible. When stressed and not trying to mislead, he used rage, intimidation, manipulation, duplicity, and threats of physical violence to motivate and influence others toward his goals. His brains were as mesmerizing to me as a fine flute to a young cobra. Here I was, trained in ethics, thinking I could change the compass setting while working for the other side.

You recognize his voice: First power without brakes. In moments, he could kill innovation, paralyze speech, and convince Americans to weigh the costs of a quick move to Costa Rica. He could turn a team of brilliant engineers, planners, architects, lawyers, salespeople, scientists, code writers, and M.B.A.'s into a schoolroom of stunned mullets.

Make no mistake: he was motivating and influencing us toward organizational goals. But the absence of respect, the paucity of encouragement, the blatant manipulation of facts—the breaching of integrity and teamwork—totally undid his effectiveness. Instead of using his great intellect to inspire teams, he used force to dispirit souls.

I felt motivated and influenced. I was motivated to leave the company and influenced to challenge the CEO's leadership to him and to the board. I did all three.

Dare we call his behaviors *leadership*? For if this is it, how in the world do we describe the high behaviors of principled and inspiring leaders, the ones who fill our higher-order needs for respect, valued labor, and selfless relationships?

I think I can make the case that leadership lives most clearly in the acts of a courageous, high-integrity leader. First, terminology.

Calling CEO Hoss's behaviors leadership is like renaming cowardice as conflict aversion or labeling tough, gutsy, rock-hard communication disciplines as touchy-feely. It's like calling a ground loop a soft landing.

If abuse, intimidation, humiliation, and rage can be called leadership, then a cold home-delivery pizza can be called a twenty-four-course Chinese banquet with five rounds of Eight Happiness Dessert.

No. Let us be honest or, at least, frank: abuse, intimidation, humiliation, and threats are illegal.

Motivating with fear and influencing with bribery are felonies. They are toxic and unprincipled. They are haunting human cultural hangovers from slavery, bondage, and serfdom.

They are not leadership any more than a great white shark in a splash pool is a canned tuna.

We can now say that the conventional leadership definition, relying on the morally ambiguous concepts of *motivation* and *influence*, is finally outdated in modern America and the increasingly relational world.

## Defining Leadership Once and for All

For thousands of years, humans have debated the meaning of leadership. In a room of a hundred executives, we could hear two hundred different definitions. Given a national uncertainty about how to lead, it is time to relieve acute polarities of the past, to harmonize existential angst over conflicting definitions, and to light a way into our new century.

I will therefore hold out no longer: I am going to uncloak the long-withheld truth about leadership.

Here is the more functional, third-power definition:

Leadership:
Ethically Inspiring Others to Be Their Best Selves
to Courageously Act for What Is Right

This is the ultimate power-punch combination that merges courage and character with people and inspiration. It's what we always need and want. We have seen it change others. When we do it, it changes us.

Applying it will improve your leading and living and produce positive Point of Decision outcomes.

# 11

# THREE ACTS OF COURAGEOUS LEADERSHIP

The great need for anyone in authority is courage.
—*Alistair Cooke*

Three acts define the courageous leader. Two stories will illuminate those behaviors for our consideration.

## Honoring All Persons

In the 1960s, the Davis campus of the University of California was internationally renowned for its agricultural college. Situated on a farming plain a hundred miles north of San Francisco, the small and friendly campus, whose rallying theme song was "Bossy Cow-Cow," had the feel of a rural town from an earlier era.

During lunch hour in the hot summer of 1969, ducks sought shade in the Putah Creek trees, and office workers heading for the quad saw a woman pacing in front of the main administration building.

Speaking imperfect English, the woman seemed to be asking passersby for money. Those that listened heard that she was asking for advice—how could she find financial help for her son?

A stream of faculty, staff, visitors, and undergrads and law students dealt with her by looking away, crossing the street, changing direction, focusing on conversations, or suddenly having a passionate curiosity about the time.

A financial aid officer named Thurn Logan stopped and asked if he might help. She burst into tears, thanking him again and again for showing her so much respect. There were then few Asians in

Davis. He thought she was Chinese, then changed his mind—she was too tall.

The woman was in fact from Shanghai, where she had learned different dialects, been educated by American missionaries, and then participated in a heroic and Homeric flight from a China torn by war and invasion. Now she struggled to understand what the kind man was saying. She'd been in America for over a decade but knew few African American people; this man's speech seemed to differ from white American dialect.

"I have son, such good boy," she said, "very smart, just learn English, but no money send him school. Please, help my son. We have daughter in China, all money go to her, get her back to family, here."

Thurn Logan was remarkable for many reasons. Relevant to this story was his disciplined honoring of all persons. This despite the fact that he had seldom received the benefits of this practice in his own life.

Thurn Logan found that the woman's son possessed great promise.

The son, David Kai Tu, was admitted that fall to UC Davis. He graduated in four years in civil engineering and earned a higher degree in engineering and an M.B.A. while mastering every sport he met. I was his college counselor, offering a service he never required.

## First Leadership Act: Honoring and Respecting All Persons

Respect is the first behavior of leadership. Respect is the human ignition switch and starter flag for principled relationships. Without unflinchingly consistent respect for all persons, leaders cannot lead and managers cannot manage.

We are often like the passersby on the UC Davis campus who unthinkingly dishonor others by looking away. Thurn Logan demonstrated the first act of leadership by respecting another—he offered his help.

To honor means to respect and esteem highly. Why do we resist this? Because we erroneously equate *respect* with *recognition*.

They're not the same. Respecting all does not mean that everyone we know receives equal rewards, responsibilities, offices, bonuses, compensation, awards, celebratory banquets and ticker tape parades.

It does mean that the lowliest performer or most challenged worker receives attention, regard, listening, and respect from courageous leaders—unconditional positive respect, or UPR. UPR is a leadership discipline. Why?

Because courageous leaders are responsible for building enduring teams. They can't do that by playing favorites based on performance, personalities, pride, or punctuality. Respect is not merit. All parties are expected to do their best, to act as a team, and to align their behaviors with the company's high core values. None of that can happen if respect is not uniformly and consistently practiced.

What do UPR, honor, and respect look like behaviorally?

- *Whole presence.* You are totally and positively present with the other person. No multitasking. No looking at the work on the desk, the monitor, your nails, your watch, or the door. No calls or interruptions.
- *Excellent body language.* Face the other person squarely. Be open. For much of American culture, this means no crossed arms or legs, no leaning back, no holding your head in your hands. (In some cultures, crossing your arms signals thoughtful reflection.) Make friendly eye contact, and when appropriate, smile. Smiling is the most powerful and encouraging function of your relational face. A smile, far from suggesting that you're imitating Goofy, declares that it's safe to talk to you. In safety and trust, magic occurs. Without them, it's back to the Middle Ages.

Not long ago, I began a coaching relationship with an executive from the Middle East. He later told me that although he was wary of being coached by an American, he decided that the arrangement could work when he saw me smile as we met. After working with managers from every continent, I have yet to encounter a time when a smile has proved to be inappropriate.

- *Careful, respectful, thoughtful listening.* Understand what is being said. Let that shape what and how you speak. Seek to *get it.*

Even if you're talking with a rival or a person you personally dislike, you are wholly and positively present. You send respectful body language, square-on, with good eye contact. You listen carefully, respectfully, thoughtfully. You do this for all persons.

Recall that research indicates that we remember 80 percent of the feelings in a conversation but only 20 percent of what was said. *How* often trumps *what.*

When I think of honor and respect, two images come to mind. First is Eleanor Roosevelt's legendary competence in communication, which was based on many developed skills. One was the ability to make the person she was with, whether a head of state or a dispossessed midwestern farmer, feel as if he or she were the most important person in the world. In such settings, possibilities occur and principles can be advanced.

Second is Charles A. Murray, whose exploits have been reported in other leadership works. Murray used to play college lacrosse, and I still see him with that big defensive stance. He's a muscular stick of ethical dynamite, made amusing by insouciance, made memorable by his principles, made lovable by a heart that pulses for ethics with a fever that most associate with venal sins.

One day, I knew Charlie had to fire one of his managers. I expected him to act quickly and decisively. I wasn't surprised when I saw the manager arrive at headquarters.

Later in the day, I saw Charlie shake hands with that individual. The man was smiling so broadly that I realized that I was completely wrong about his professional jeopardy.

"I'm sorry to say," said Charlie later, "I had to let 'Joe' go."

Yet Charlie had treated him with the heartfelt warmth that I had thought was only reserved for high performers—not to mention a person being fired for underperformance. I had witnessed an unforgettable example of unconditional positive respect.

Using honor and UPR, courageous leaders absolutely refuse to split their organizations into a three-class bell curve of loved favorites, banished Siberians, and the forgettable midlanders. Courageous leaders honor all persons. Even when asking an exec to leave for lack of character or competence, they are faultlessly respectful.

On the other hand, the courageous leader clearly and decisively differentiates between people in rewards, recognitions, promotions, assignments, and bonuses. These do not reflect respect—they reflect merit. Holding to this difference requires discipline, and being disciplined requires courage. Don't be deceived: respect is a tough and demanding leadership skill. It takes backbone. It isn't touchy-feely or warm and fuzzy.

Let's talk about "soft leadership skills." I submit to you that they are in fact hard. If they were easy, everyone would have them. Further, "touchy-feely" is not a way to characterize professional relationships. It implies an emotional and physical closeness that is inappropriate in nonfamily relationships between adults. Touchy-feely has little play in most professional settings except, perhaps, massage therapy and Greco-Roman wrestling.

If we label courageous communication as "soft" or "touchy-feely," we are actually protecting our negative tendencies and our worst habits while simultaneously sabotaging professional collegiality, the power of emotions, and the responsibility to manage them. These are unhelpful labels that distance us from principled behaviors.

Respect is the leadership discipline that invites teamwork and the growth of a leadership bench. Its opposites—favoritism and rationed regard—produce many of our organizational heartaches.

Giving respect, particularly when we don't feel like it, is a learned skill. It's also fundamental to effective leading.

Coach Tony and Major Schwarzkopf, respectively, once saw a kid and a cadet in need of massive calories and moral development. Even though my cowardice made my coach recoil in shock and my laziness evoked dismay in my mentor, they both managed to resist tossing me out the nearest window. Instead, I suspect, they marshaled all their will power and high-spined discipline to treat me with courageous respect.

Had I "earned" any respect? Absolutely not. I instead embodied nearly everything they wished to disrespect.

Of course, it wasn't about me. It was about them and their ability to lead, develop, and team up with a widely diverse group of individuals to impart high core values.

Any one could have scorned me; it took steel backbones and courageous relationalism to challenge, develop, and respect all others. It took backbones of steel to overcome the feelings that lead to judgment instead of assessment and development instead of sockeyed cursing.

Leaders respect and appreciate all, reward many, and fire a few.

## Second Leadership Act: Encouraging and Supporting Others

To become a director in pre-WorldCom MCI, senior manager Mike Keegan[1] had to pass personal interviews with both a C-level executive and a division president. Not all senior execs look as good as they can think, and some resemble *Seinfeld*'s Kramer after a lightning strike.

But the two broad-shouldered executives Mike had to face were dynamos in pressed Dockers, power hitters in the Fortune 100 ballpark, dealmakers, rainmakers, and beau ideals for headhunters and rivals. Corporate power in the flesh, they looked the role. Payton Neelum, the C-level, had an incisive intellect. John Gerdelman, president of Network Services, was known for excellence in results.

Keegan met Payton Neelum first, at the Colorado Springs airport. Neelum shook Keegan's hand and said, "I've heard you're good."

They entered a limousine. Inside, Keegan, a Phi Beta Kappa and a highly experienced manager, prepared for tough questions.

Neelum punched numbers and talked to his brokers during the entire ride from the airport. At the office, Neelum detailed his vision. It turned out to be a familiar message Keegan had already memorized. Neelum asked no questions.

A female exec entered, and Neelum openly studied her chest. The meeting ended when Neelum abruptly made another phone call.

MCI was in merger talks with WorldCom's Bernie Ebbers, and Payton Neelum was a key player. MCI had a teamwork culture, but Neelum was famous for being a brilliantly quick and highly aggressive lone wolf.

Standing in the hallway, Keegan reflected on Payton Neelum's focus on his stock portfolio, his lack of engagement, his lack of respect for a female colleague. He felt that Neelum had dealt with them as if they were mildly bothersome insects. They were in merger talks, and Keegan thought, *If Payton Neelum has a big voice in them, we're in big trouble.*

The second interview was with the president of MCI Network Services, John Gerdelman.

"Could you pick me up at the airport?" Gerdelman had asked Keegan. Punctual Mike Keegan exited the cab. *Unbelievably, he was half an hour late.*

"I had never been late, ever," he said to me later. "I panicked. Waiting by the terminal stood Gerdelman and his bags. I mean, this was the president! He was smiling as I leaped from the cab."

"Hi, Mike," said Gerdelman. "How are you? Thanks for meeting me. Is this our taxi?"

"Mr. Gerdelman, I'm so sorry I'm late. I thought you had a limo." John smiled, "No, no limo." He loaded his own luggage. In the cab, he looked at Mike. "I always love Colorado Springs."

For the next two hours, Gerdelman asked about Keegan's background and passions. He asked about values conflicts, top issues, challenges, success inhibitors. Gerdelman listened and took notes. Then he said something that Mike Keegan says he will remember until the day he dies.

"Mike, I came out here to do this interview for one reason. When there's a problem, I want you to come to me so I can help you solve it."

Although MCI was a great company, Keegan had never heard such words. "Thank you," he said, surprised by the depth of his feelings.

Soon thereafter, Keegan, now a director, received a team of project engineers who nervously presented evidence that a major, high-level project was in irreversible failure. Keegan immediately told his senior VP.

"That can't be true," said the senior VP. "But if it is, fix it."

"It can't be fixed," said Keegan

"Sure it can." Perhaps the news was too painful to face. In any event, the VP continued to pour resources into what clearly was a write-off.

Keegan remembered John Gerdelman's words. The project was outside Gerdelman's area of operation, but he took Keegan's call, reviewed the evidence, and agreed with the analysis. He then privately conferred with the senior VP and offered suggestions. MCI shut down the project and averted a $200 million catastrophe with a key client.

Courageous leadership is muscle that permits character-based leaders to act rightly regardless of pressure and changing circumstances.

Payton Neelum was educated, brilliant, and competent. But courage and humility are features of *character*, not *intellect*. Large smarts do not mean moral courage. Neelum possessed the standing to provide inspirational encouragement and support principled behaviors that would have inspired teamwork and harmony. To use a Chinese expression, his generosity of spirit would inspire others to tell his story.

Instead, Payton Neelum focused on himself. Coach Tony once said that a person can knock himself on the head, but he can't clap himself on the back or kick himself in the rear. For those services, we need others. Neelum needed to inspire others and chose not to.

As an MCI leadership consultant in those days, I saw a man earnestly speaking to an employee inside her cubicle. Her neighbors were trying to listen without appearing rude. I noticed the intensity of the man's communication and the matching focus of those around him.

I asked an engineer who the man was.

"That's John Gerdelman, network president," said the engineer. "You know that he spends a major part of every visit talking one on one with employees, by name? He has twenty thousand people in his world, but he thanks secretaries, coders, managers, clerks, and consultants across the whole company. Outside the network. He's always thanking people who do the work on the line."

John Gerdelman demonstrated encouragement by unconditionally respecting and individually recognizing and thanking people throughout the company. He demonstrated support by immediately responding to Mike Keegan's need for right action. Gerdelman is now chairman of the board for Intelliden, but people at MCI still talk of him with affection, appreciation, and admiration. Mention his name, and hard-nosed engineers will take a deep breath and become wistful.

Courageous leading begins with *honoring all persons* and ends in *correcting wrongs*. In the middle are the behaviors of *encouraging and supporting*.

## Encouragement

Encouragement is relational. Collegial reinforcement, giving courage, the high power of camaraderie, the presence of approval and hope—these are the strengths of humanity and relationships of the third power.

I have seen the power of encouragement as a parent and as an executive. The power of encouragement allowed me to survive and sustains me today.

Encouragement is huge but often absent. Kouzes and Posner report in *Encouraging the Heart* that a whopping 98 percent of execs think they would perform better with encouragement.[2] Yet few get the encouragement that we've organically needed since drawing our first breath.

Coach Tony guided and modeled by building a CR,—a *courage-based relationship*. His guts gave him the discipline to stay with me even as his gorge was rising. Encouragement is the giving of courage. It is supporting, reinforcing, and rallying people to right behaviors, to high core values and excellent standards, and to courage itself. We do this first by demonstrating courage. We do it also by knowing our people—watching, coaching, and developing them so that we can instantly affirm their rightful behaviors and their demonstrated competencies.

Second, we make our need for and pride in each person crystal clear. Charlie Murray showed this in his behaviors, moods, language, and habits as a leader, which managed to convey "I need you. I respect you. I'm very proud of you."

Encouragement can't be misused. If words are used to support wrongful behaviors, that's not encouragement. It's abetting and manipulating.

Major Schwarzkopf encouraged by spending individual, one-on-one (CR$_1$) time with me and with other academically challenged cadets. He created an ethical relationship based on helping and guiding, and it changed my life. He could have spent his time with the Rhodes scholarship candidates and the All-American football players; instead, he chose to assist those with a busted wing, a weak spirit, self-doubts, or lamentable study skills.

This doesn't mean that Major Schwarzkopf beamed brightly at bridging diagrams that may yet represent the most preposterous force vectors in the history of all stupid diagrams. Rather, he placed a sincere red X across my solution, told me to see him later, and moved on to the next cadet.

When I fled the ring like an Olympic jumping bean and smacked into the unseen wall, Coach Tony did not laud me. *Au contraire*. He instantly, affirmatively, and clearly corrected my errors in judgment and movement. Nonverbally, he made clear his feelings about my action.

Encouragement arises from the heart of the encourager as opposed to the recipient's need for affirmation. Encouragement is not self-esteem. Encouragement is given for progress toward the development of high core values, behaviors, habits, skills, and competencies. It does not mean that it should be given for failures, but it must be delivered for true effort.

It *does* mean that the coach and mentor continued to encourage my effort, my *try*, and to support my potential success with teaching, tutoring, and occasional respectfully creative oaths.

Of John Gerdelman's many gifts, two appear to inspire the greatest number of stories around the campfire: encouragement and courage. His encouraging line workers, one on one, and his courage in addressing institutional mistakes have become the stuff of legend. These interactions occurred without the use of authority or rewards. They were rich in respect, encouragement, support, and acting for what is right.

Encouragement and courage have exponential and transformational power. In leadership programs, we often begin the first day with ropes and other outdoor education exercises. These allow executives to *encourage* each other on the features and to lend actual physical *support* to ensure safety in accomplishment.

"Something happens," said a member of the ISEC team, "when one of us is on a ropes feature and every person—*every* person—cheers him on. It changes how we relate. I think, for a moment, it changes our chemistry. It lets us support each other back in the office."

The power of encouragement is great and immediately available to all. It seems that we choose not to encourage at our own risk.

## Support

Coach Tony supported me by inviting me (there was no saying no) to repeat Introductory Boxing. This supported me by keeping me alive long enough to reach Intermediate Boxing. He developed my abilities by dedicating personal time, bag time, and ring time to my development.

Major Schwarzkopf supported me by pouring extra instruction into our bottom-crawling section. We were assigned to twelve-person sections based on our grades in that course, with Section 1 consisting of the top performers. I believe we were in Solid Mechanics Section 1,983. Spending his time and energy, one on one, he patiently showed me how to calculate moment arms and draft accurate diagrams. Under his tutelage, I became good.

The last leadership action is the capstone.

## Third Leadership Act: Challenging Wrongs

You can feel John Gerdelman's positive energy across a crowded room. Some of that quality has to be inborn, but he says that his leadership development and his caring for people began when he started working at construction sites in St. Louis at the age of fourteen.

Gerdelman cares about people. This is no accident of nature—it's an intentionally cultivated discipline.

"When you're fourteen," he pointed out, "you learn what it's like to be managed, and you learn what it feels like to be mistreated. It was a great learning period. You ask me, where else did I learn to take care of people?

"I started out as a Navy line officer. I had a great chief. He really coached me. Said that every time I stepped onto the flight line, I had to know what my people were doing and be prepared, that I couldn't know unless I got down on the lines and hoses, into the trenches, with them.

"I learned to shake my people's hands, to see how they're doing. To be with them. A carrier flight deck is very active. Safety's no joke because it's a dangerous place. You learn to really care for people.

"Later, I was a pilot on the USS *Eisenhower*'s maiden voyage. There were thirty-two aviators in our squadron. The separation from our families was very hard on the group; sixteen of us ended up divorced. It was a double lesson about taking care of your people and being intentional about your family."

Less important to him was his desire to fly fighters—a privilege he earned by being at the top of his class—and the different honor of being the first ensign to pilot the electronically overendowed E6B.

Gerdelman learned principled behaviors in everything he did, from playing team-focused fullback at William and Mary ("You learn that everyone depends on everyone else") to working for American Hospital Supply and its high-tempo sales culture. At AHS headquarters, he learned the intricacies of corporate accounting while observing a top executive break almost every rule he encountered.

"It was a great lesson for me. I didn't like how this man was operating. I resisted his habits. I was relieved when he was caught and left the firm. I learned that you can get ahead by cheating, but eventually, you're going to lose."

He learned as a naval aviator the organic nature of commitment. Once on a flight path to land on the pitching deck of a carrier, there's no backing out, no weaseling to the side, no room for a change of heart. The entire ship depends on your doing it right and doing it true.

"I needed all of that when Jerry Taylor hired me at MCI. It was 1994, and MCI's network was the absolute worst in the industry. MCI had huge, continuous network failures, collapses, and breaks. It was a disaster with the network going down every day and customers leaving in waves." MCI was at its Point of Decision.

"I reminded myself that I have to stay with it, fly the airplane, stay with the people, and help them repair the network.

"It came down to minute details, the small things. Helping the people track down the sources of failure. Supporting them with their needs. Being with them during the breaks and helping them with the repairs. The people did it—in less than a year, we went from bottom to top. You have to keep flying the plane with everything you have."

Unstated by Gerdelman is the miracle turnaround executed by the people for whom he was responsible. However, its dramatic success would now bring the company to a new Point of Decision.

## Addressing Wrongs in Others and in the Institution

"WorldCom had just purchased MCI. I was meeting with Scott Sullivan and Bernie Ebbers in Mississippi, where WorldCom was headquartered."

Ebbers had a great presence, but it didn't take long before Gerdelman found himself saying, "Those are intricate schemes, but you can't write off losses and change depreciation schedules that way." He drilled down in the level of detail and explained the consequences to his new boss. Through all the numbers and the fog, the opportunities for wealth and the chances for catastrophe, Gerdelman saw the truth.

Gerdelman could tell by the expressions on their faces and the ensuing silence that Ebbers and Sullivan didn't expect him—known for engineering a national network recovery—to catch the highly sophisticated ramifications of their intended creative accounting or, having seen it, to openly challenge it.

But catch it and then call them on it he did.

Ebbers looked at Gerdelman, waiting for him to back down. Gerdelman stayed with the plane and kept it on its true path. More words were exchanged. Gerdelman repeated his dire concerns. Impasse.

"I was walking back with MCI CEO Jerry Taylor from the meeting. We were on a gravel path that led back to our hotel room."

Gerdelman had crunched the numbers in the meetings with the new president and CFO, to no avail; now he heard a similar music beneath his feet that comes from shoe leather sliding on small, slippery rocks.

"I said to myself, *I'm not going to do this. I'm not going to do anything unethical, thank God.*

"I turned to Jerry Taylor. Jerry was my mentor, the guy who had hired me to realign MCI's network. He's a straight-up guy.

"I said to him, 'This doesn't smell right.'

"Jerry nodded. 'I agree,' he said. The next day, both of us gave notice."

Meanwhile, the new corporate direction was becoming more evident.

It's not clear whether Payton Neelum, the other MCI exec who had done the director interviews, saw the moral imperative—the right path in the fog of many choices. If he saw the truth, it apparently lacked the same personal impact on his core values that it provided to Gerdelman and Taylor.

Neelum continued to participate in managing the merger with WorldCom and contributed to the design that led to catastrophe and the largest bankruptcy in U.S. economic history. His desire for wealth was understandable, but his pursuit of it was unprincipled in its excessiveness and single-mindedness.

John Gerdelman recognized the present, understood the future, and spoke candidly about what it foretold. He directly challenged the accounting practices that would cripple a fine organization.

It is clear that his accounting counsel was not heeded, and he accordingly left WorldCom long before it imploded. He became a highly successful CEO for a major firm in a related industry, leading another turnaround that saved an enterprise, thousands of jobs, and millions in savings and retirement accounts.

We later learned that WorldCom had misreported revenues. Its $11 billion in debt set another negative ethics record as its stock dropped from $56 to $0. Payton Neelum went on, in very rapid succession, to become CEO of three different firms and was let go by the last company after being at the helm less than a year.

Bernie Ebbers was convicted of fraud, compelled to forfeit his wealth, and sentenced to twenty-five years in prison.

All executives and all organizations face Points of Decision.

At Whirlpool, Mike Thienemen faced an array of choices. He could've opted to deny the causes of Whirlpool's profitability gap or to cover for executives who had failed in character. He chose instead to continue to perform the three leadership acts:

- He respected those without courage or forthrightness, but he did not agree with them.

- He supported and encouraged all employees to act rightly.
- He challenged wrong behaviors.

The personal and institutional outcomes were identically desirable.

## Correcting Wrongs in Oneself

Even as an undergraduate and young student leader, David Kai Tu had a startling ability to act spontaneously for what was right. He spoke truthfully and fearlessly to suspicious vice-chancellors, worried deans, resistant professors, and angry activist student leaders. Today, blessed with a wonderful family, David Kai Tu is president of the high-tech firm DCL and a stealthy philanthropist in education and the arts.

He's never forgotten his mother's generous courage and high principles, Thurn Logan's thoughtful and unconditional positive respect for his mother, or the fine public university that gave him his professional chance. Like most people who act for principle, David doesn't think of himself as courageous.

"I don't know, Gus," he said, "I haven't stopped a bullet." I know if he had to, he would. He doesn't use his corporate title and only tolerates it in this book because I suggested that it could be helpful.

It is very much like him, as a teacher and mentor to others, to offer stories that reflect his humility. "I was a VP," says David, "in a national real estate and construction firm. I was in a situation where I was verbally inappropriate to one of the administrative assistants. Worse, I did the yelling and the showing of my temper in front of her peers.

"I did it because my position got to my ego. Even as I was doing it, I knew it was wrong, but I didn't stop. Later, I couldn't stop thinking about what I had done. Troubled by my inappropriateness, I met with the assistant in private and apologized.

"I then gathered all the parties who had witnessed my misbehavior. Again, I apologized to her, and then I apologized to the others."

Courageous leading *begins* with honoring all persons, regardless of rank, status, education, or power. The least experienced person instinctively respects people with rank. It takes courage to equally honor all persons, favorites or not.

Leading *ends* with correcting wrongs—particularly in oneself.

David recognized his failure.

Egotism and greed guide our behaviors when our private needs overwhelm our conscience, judgment, and principles.

This is amazingly paradoxical, because when our needs drive our behaviors, we're guaranteeing ourselves that those primary human needs will go unmet. We'll be without genuine affection, caring relationships, and principled interactions. This makes for enduring misery. Under pressure, we forget this truth and harm ourselves and others.

Ever since we were children, we disliked kids who were selfish, self-centered, and greedy. We didn't trust them.

Yet we evolve when we climb out of the primordial soup of base survival. We become better people by supporting others according to principle and not whim. Since we were little, we admired people who were generous and brave. We still do.

We are our best selves when we champion high principles and demonstrate courage for those who need advocates. This is common human knowledge, for we all learned about heroes when we were young. Older now, we are in position to leverage that knowledge. When we stop fearing the possibilities of emotional loss, we gain.

Challenging wrongs, the last element of courageous leadership, comes last because it's often the most demanding behavior.

It has four parts:

1. Discern right from wrong.
2. Act for what is right regardless of risk.
3. Stop wrongs in oneself and challenge wrongs in others.
4. Follow through so that wrongs are not repeated.

Chris Kay of IntegWare wanted to both discipline and protect his underperforming COO. Chris respected and supported Will Sampson, demonstrating the first three acts of courageous leadership. When the evidence became clear, Chris discerned right from wrong. He then practiced the third act and the third power by courageously facing his own challenge (resistance to conflict) and addressing Will's issues (character challenges and resulting substandard behaviors). Finally, he took steps to ensure no repetition of either his resistance or his failure to screen everyone for courage competence. The personal and institutional outcomes were identically admirable.

To succeed, the third act of leadership, having the courage to challenge wrongs, requires the presence of the first two acts—honoring and respecting others and supporting and encouraging them. Courage without respect of all others becomes unthinking brashness; courage without support of others becomes grandstanding egotism.

John Gerdelman of Intelliden excels in courage. Beginning as a teen, he discerned right from wrong. He recognized his tendency to be unprepared on an active flight deck and to be unintentional in watching out for his people, and he exchanged those tendencies for disciplined, values-centered leadership behaviors.

At WorldCom, he respectfully addressed wrongs that he observed and took rightful follow-up action.

David Kai Tu of DCL excels in courage. But any strength, unchecked, has the capacity to become a weakness. One day, David's great drive to produce results surfaced in the form of inappropriate anger.

David saw his personal failing. Instead of denying it or blaming the object of his wrongful behavior, he courageously convicted himself of the error.

He then apologized, which, by coupling conscience with action, allowed him to decisively correct the behavior.

Courage is readily available to us all. Each of us can express courage today.

If you study Intelliden, Whirlpool, Kimberley-Clark, Kaiser Permanente, DCL, IntegWare—any principled firm—you'll see decision-

making cycles employing universal respect, encouragement and support, and the courage to correct wrongs.

When those institutions face Points of Decision, they are already trained, educated, seasoned, and equipped to test their best
principles against the most difficult and painful challenges. They
are ready to convert crisis into a triumph of principle.

# 12

## COURAGEOUS PROBLEM SOLVING: THE BLACK BOX

Courage faces fear and thereby masters it.
Cowardice represses fear and is thereby mastered
by it.

—*Martin Luther King Jr.*

New York. The business: a large financial institution. The senior exec: Tom Kenner. Broad-shouldered, immaculate, finely casual with a suggestion of the oleaginous. I'm a consultant to his firm, reporting to the COO, and have been interviewing him about the company's biggest concern: his feud with another VP named Mark Crew.

I've told Tom that our interview could create discomfort. After half an hour, I'm at the key question: "Have you ever been unethical with Mark?"

A snort. "Mark is the liar. He's backstabbed me for twenty years and grandstands on others' work. If Mark Crew had a pet howler monkey with a red hat on his lap, you couldn't tell them apart."

"*Twenty years* of antagonism. Tom? That's a long time. I hear Mark's concerns about your accuracy with numbers."

He blew out air. "It is the nature of our business. Next question."

"Have you ever been unethical with Mark?"

"He hasn't earned my respect. How could I be unethical?"

"Did you ever give him or his people the wrong numbers?"

"Come on! How could I lie? I don't talk to him."

"Your people talk to his people? No? Well, do they get along?"

Tom Kenner shook his head. "I don't think so."

"Tom, you solve hairy problems involving complex interactions between foreign governments, the International Monetary Fund, and multinationals. What stops you from fixing a key relationship with a colleague?"

"Frankly, Gus, he's not worth it."

"What would make it worthwhile? Can you estimate what your feud with Mark has cost the firm in its core values? In efficiency, quality, teamwork, cross-functional unity, income, customer confidence?"

He tapped his fingers. "That calls for a gross simplification."

I smiled. "Well, then I could understand it better."

"Crew is an idiot. I fear I'll disgrace myself and attack him."

Head shake. "You're too smart for that. So why not solve it?"

Tom sighed, then leaned forward. "People think I'm a tough, hard negotiator. But I don't like conflict. I guess that's why I avoid Mark Crew."

I nodded. "Can you tell me more about that?"

"Simple. I don't like messes. Conflicts are messy."

"Can I share this? I see the huge resistance to making peace with Mark. Bigger than simply detesting him. What do you think that is?"

"You're wrong. I simply detest him. End of argument."

"And your detesting him trumps the firm's needs for teamwork?"

"Gus, I didn't say that."

"OK, that was me talking. Did you ever hear of *communication triangulation*?" He shook his head.

"It's you telling me about Mark instead of you talking to Mark."

"What's your point?"

"What's less messy: speaking to Mark or to third parties?"

He laughed. "It wouldn't matter if you knew Mark Crew."

"Can you see how telling customers about Mark makes things messy for the firm?"

"In theory."

"In theory, what's best: solving problems or avoiding conflict?"

"I love how you gloss tough problems into simplicities."

I grinned. "We consultants use simplicities, don't we?"

He sighed. "Gus, who sent you to do this? The president didn't."

"I'm not so sure. The firm's entering into a Point of Decision—an inflection point—with his impending retirement. He thinks your feud with Mark is a threat to stability and profitability. I agreed. So here I am."

A hint of a grin. "You're really doing this on your own."

I laughed. "I hope not! It won't work that way. I'm going to ask both of you to talk directly to each other. Not just once, but from now on. Regardless of what you think of each other.

"He could be Rasputin dragging chains, but here's the condition: no more communication triangulation. Can you imagine such a thing?"

"Not really."

"Tom, thank you very much for your time. I know you'll help me with Mark Crew."

## Mark Crew's View of Tom Kenner

He is precise with a quick smile, a high laugh, megadynes of brain power, a hint of vulnerability, and a habit of pouring sugar in coffee. He quickly accused Kenner of fudging numbers for twenty years and of being as trustworthy as an escaped convict in a gun shop.

I asked Mark Crew, "You ever act unethically with Tom Kenner?"

"No. I have not. I am not the one who's ethically challenged. I am not the one who takes kickbacks, free vacations, and inappropriate gifts. I'm not the one who forges documents."

"Those are very dramatic issues," I said. "May I ask this? Is it ethical to gossip? To tell stories behind Kenner's back?"

He shook his head. "No, it isn't. I guess I do it, *sometimes*."

"What do you think about *sometimes* not being principled?"

"It happens. You're talking about that *triangulation* thing, right?" Quietly, he said, "Well, I do it. I guess that'd disappoint my mentor."

I leaned forward. "Why would Sy not like that?"

"Sy believed in direct dialogue. Polite but direct."

"That's very wise. Mark, Tom says you take undeserved credit."

"Tom only believes in himself and a double Stoli martini."

"You've never taken undeserved credit?"

Anger. "That's exactly what I'm saying."

"OK. Then he's mistaken."

"Tom often is."

Earlier, I had asked each of them, "When's the last time the two of you shared a civil word with each other?"

Tom Kenner had said, "When snakes danced the hokey-pokey."

Mark Crew had said, "Never."

"When's the last time a superior told you two to make up?"

They couldn't remember. Never. That was impressive: twenty years of letting institutional courage decay in a back warehouse while senior execs slugged it out on the schoolyard.

I asked them to meet me at the Waldorf Astoria.

Tom Kenner and Mark Crew said they'd think about it. They said it the way people used to say they'd like to live in Siberia.

I had visited the Waldorf as a lean West Point cadet, associating the cool marble and rectangular pillars with freedom and food. Even now, I still stretch my neck and smack my lips near Oscar's brasserie. A man paused, looking as if I needed the Heimlich maneuver.

The firm had reserved a room that would seat the World Bank. The table resembled the one at which Charles Foster and Mary Kane ate, miles apart, in *Citizen Kane*. This would allow Tom Kenner and Mark Crew to be as far apart as possible while remaining in the United States. I prepped flipcharts and lighting. I prepared mentally and emotionally.

Both execs, drilled to global punctuality, were stylishly late.

Before we consider the meeting that resulted, let's understand the dynamics:

What was the unmentioned force that drove these dialogues?

It was conflict aversion. Here were two smart, tough, and successful executives who were absolutely stymied by the inability to resolve deeply held differences. It seemed to both of them that it would be best to criticize the other behind his back while avoiding face-to-face contact.

When we don't exercise our character muscles, when we don't deeply discern anticipated and habitual actions, we can end up with options that *seem to be good*. That's how we ended up with conflict aversion. It seemed to be a good idea at the time. But it never appeared to be a great idea.

Conflict aversion is the organizational bubonic plague of our times. It is cowardice wearing a smart, politically correct hat. The hat allows it entry into all human organizations, where it befuddles, ensnarls, and twists communication. It turns dialogue from a leadership tool into a virus to which only a precious few are immune.

Perhaps I'm being extreme: conflict aversion makes infinite sense if you are living in a totalitarian state in which coughing at the wrong time means a death sentence for you and your family. Conflict aversion is also precisely the appropriate option if you're considering fighting a brown bear with a toothpick.

But in an open society and in quadruped-free organizations, it's illogical and tragic for a free people to operate from fear of feelings.

It's wrong to adopt fear and avoidance as life principles. It's like using our brains and experience to build marble shrines to cowardice.

In such a shrine, we're convinced it would be better to be cowardly than to appear unpopular or alone. Here we're asked to do what appears to be good and assured that doing it is OK if we make a habit of it.

When Tom Kenner resolved to not deal with Mark Crew, it was ostensibly because of Mark's faults. In fact, I believe it was a reflection of Tom's issues. Tom's investment in personal pride and his fear that Mark had convincing evidence of Tom's lack of ethics led him to avoid Mark.

On the other hand, I believe that Mark Crew refused to deal with Tom Kenner because he feared Tom's intimidating behaviors and was guided by an overwhelming sense that being right required that he scorn the other person. Frustrated that the president hadn't sanctioned Tom for his lack of ethics, Mark insisted on carrying out his own version of punishment of the accused.

When such habits become entrenched over years, we need to use an approach I call the Black Box.

This model is built on the courageous behavioral strategies we learned in Chapters Seven and Eight. The Black Box, like all tools in this book, relies on high core values.

## Aligning Behaviors with Core Values

They entered warily. I greeted them warmly. Each stared fixedly at me as if the other person, like the Seven Cities of Cibola, never existed.

"Good morning to you both! Mark, do you trust Tom as a colleague?"

Mark Crew drew back as if slapped. A big shake of the head.

I turned to Tom. "Tom, do you trust Mark as a colleague?"

"Clearly," he said tersely, "you understand that I don't."

"Teamwork is one of your core values. Can we work on it together?"

"I admit I'm curious," said Tom, "about what you can do."

"I am as well," said Mark, pouring sugar in his coffee.

I said, "Your responsibility is to form professional and collegial relationships. Today, our objective is to create civility. Next time, we'll work on collegiality. Do you have questions about purpose or today's objective?"

No one spoke. I smiled. "Let me start with an easy, lighthearted question. How much do you get paid for fighting each other?"

"Restate the question," snapped Tom Kenner, adjusting cuffs.

"Fair enough. Each of you routinely criticizes the other. Not to each other's face, but to others, all over the firm, even to corporate customers and consultants. You scuttle each other's initiatives. This takes a big effort! It takes time and resources. How much are you getting paid to do this?"

"You once told us that sarcasm is hostility," said Mark Crew.

"You're right. Please forgive my tone. But it's a real question."

They both eventually said, *I guess they're not paying us to fight.*

"The president hasn't intervened. He's afraid one or both of you will quit, and he needs both of you, particularly with his impending step-down. What stops you from making peace? What are you afraid of?"

Silence, followed by more silence. Both checked the time.

I said, "Once I was in a feud. I was afraid that if I tried to make up, I'd look like I was wrong and weak, and the other guy could laugh at my offer. I ended up being trapped by my own fears."

I smiled. Finally, infinitesimal head nods.

"Is it the same for you two? Fear is our friend?" Again, silence.

"Does that apply to you? Tom?" A visible head nod. "Mark?" A nod.

"Is fear an adequate, or a good, reason to not act as a leader?"

*No,* they said.

"Gentlemen, don't look now; you just agreed." I beamed as if I had won a double-decker ice-cream cone in July. They looked like they would personally have to pay back the losses in the last corporate collapse.

## Naming the Issue

"The issue is fear. Not fear of big things but of small things.

"We fear looking bad, even in our own minds. We fear hurt pride, repercussions from genuine discussions, being wrong, looking out of step, seeming awkward, being isolated. Not big things. Small ones. This stops us from acting courageously and therefore wisely.

"So I have another leader's tool to deal with that. The Black Box. What's a black box?"

"It's a flight recorder," said Mark Crew, happy with the change in topic. "It tells the National Transportation Safety Board the probable cause of an airplane crash. It has two parts: a communication unit and a mechanical performance unit."

"And usually, the cause is pilot error," said Tom Kenner. "Or a mechanical or design failure. Or an independent intervening event."

"Right! The Black Box is a diagnostic tool. It tells us why we crashed and gives prescriptive hints about how to avoid crashing tomorrow.

"When a relationship crashes and burns, like yours, it's *always* human error. There are three usual suspects."

I turned to the chart.

## The Three Main Causes of Relationship Crashes

1. Failure to honor and respect all

2. Failure to encourage and support others

3. Failure to challenge wrongs

"These are the specific behaviors of being self-centered, greedy, inconsiderate, and abusive. People who exhibit these behaviors are the kind you don't want to hire, marry into your family, or have as a neighbor. Remember the floating bloody dagger in the mind of Macbeth? That's the image you should conjure up whenever you're going to talk badly about someone behind the person's back.

"We have a tool to uncover the daggers in our conduct—the Black Box." I turned the sheet.

"You took off together in the same high-performance aircraft, and then you fought. For twenty years, you've kept up the feud. So it should come as no surprise that your flight—your professional relationship—is a smoking crash scene, right?" A smile. "Now we dig through the wreckage. We get the Black Box. It's beat-up. We open it up and check the three assessment displays of a busted relationship: respect all persons, encourage and support others, and challenge wrongs. Why these performance indicators?"

"They're the three courageous leadership acts," said Mark, remembering the recent overview class on courageous leadership.

"Right! Wisdom has distilled a million human behaviors of influencing, motivating, and inspiring down to three that describe the best leaders: respect for all, encouragement and support, and courage to challenge wrongs. They give us principled relationships, productivity, and moral integrity."

## First Crash Cause:
## Failure to Honor and Respect All

Mark and Tom had taken the classes on courageous communication and leadership. This is what I reviewed for them:

Courageous leaders do three things and do them well. The first is respecting all persons; the other leadership acts—giving encouragement and support and challenging wrongs—build on it. So when we have a relational crash, respect is the first performance behavior we check.

To respect is to value—to be concerned for the other. It means not violating or disregarding the person. It is not friendship; it's a strict discipline of leadership, regardless of feelings; it's unconditional positive respect (UPR).

Even if you're talking with a rival, you are wholly present. You use respectful body language and good eye contact. You listen carefully, respectfully, and thoughtfully. You do this for all persons.

Recalling this, Tom and Mark were as responsive as the Sphinx.

"What happens when you're inconsistent in respecting others?"

"Respect has to be earned," said Tom quickly. Mark agreed. *They had forgotten the key truth of respect because we all do.*

I said, "OK. Let's say one of you has earned more respect from me today than the other. How would that affect our work?"

"One of us does better," said Tom. "It's the nature of our work."

"Our work would suffer," said Mark.

"Correct. What would an observer think of my conduct?" I asked.

Mark remembered. "He'd think you play favorites, cause splits."

"That's right. Each time the favored person spoke, I'd agree enthusiastically. Whenever the other person spoke, I'd ignore him or disprove his points. Where would we be after a month of that?"

Tom shrugged.

"This is what we know, and this knowledge is important: we emphasize respect as the first leadership act. Without it, we break down.

"But we keep confusing respect with trust and rewards. They're not the same. Each has different dynamics and different functions.

"Respect is not trust. Trust *has* to be earned through courageous conduct and demonstrated character. Character is sustained courage. We can *respect* everyone, but we can't *trust* everyone.

"For example, you guys don't trust each other. But that's spread into disrespect. That throws sand in the company's gears.

"Respect is not promotions and bonuses. Those are earned through competence, effort, merit, and demonstrated character. A leader honors all persons but rewards only principled performance.

"What does respect look like?" I stood by the flipchart. Between them, they managed to say, *listening, being fair, diplomatic*.

"Right. Respect is listening, fairness, civility. They are learned skills. *Leaders respect and appreciate all, reward many, and fire a few.*

"Respect is a tough and demanding leadership skill. It isn't being weak. It's the exact opposite of avoidance. It takes personal strength; it requires rigorous practice. It has been the leadership response to all forms of human oppression."

I asked, "What happens to a firm when execs play favorites?"

"You get cliques and factions," said Mark.

"That's just politics," said Tom. "It's life. They're natural."

"And as dysfunctional as the Mafia running the Red Cross. Do cliques and factions help or hurt teams and profits?"

They eventually agreed that cliques hurt profits.

"Think of it! If you two added your work together, it'd double your output. Instead, you subtract from yourself and then from each other. That's *millions* in losses every year, times twenty years. Tell me if I'm wrong." Silence.

"The respect indicator in our Black Box goes from zero to nine. I want you to assess your UPR for each other, your not interfering, violating, disrespecting the other. Write down the number that describes your behavior in this category with the other." They did.

"What's our next suspect for causing relationships to flame out?"

Mark looked at the chart. "Failure to encourage and support others."

"What does that mean?" They knew but were silent.

## Second Crash Cause:
## Failure to Encourage and Support Others

"Encouragement is relational. It is collegiality, camaraderie. It is giving courage, approval, and hope. It's what makes life good. Ninety-eight percent of execs say they'd perform better with encouragement.

"Support is resources: people, time, data, funding, meals, health plans, work-life balance. To sum up: support is management and values.

"*Encouragement* is relationships. It is leadership and values.

"Bust either, and crashing starts. Write the number to rate your support and encouragement of the other, to create teamwork."

## Third Crash Cause: Failure to Challenge Wrongs

"The third suspect for causing crashes is a lack of courage when facing wrongs in yourself, in others, or in institutions."

Ethics begins with an awareness of others; by definition, a true sociopath can't honor others or live honorably.

It's time for executives to recognize how a fear of pierced pride produces demoralization and lousy organizational outcomes, because it inadvertently leads us into behaviors of avoidance.

I turned to the sheet and reminded the men of the four steps to courageously challenging wrongs.

1. Discern right from wrong.

2. Act for what is right regardless of risk.

3. Stop wrongs in oneself and challenge wrongs in others.

4. Follow through so that wrongs are not repeated.

Looking at it, Tom Kenner stood and paced; Mark Crew got up for more coffee.

Looking at courage changes us. Even looking at it on paper carries an interior impact.

The Black Box helps us understand why a relationship has crashed. The usual suspects: failure in respect, support, or challenging wrongs.

"Gentlemen, please give yourself a number for this behavior in your relationship with the other." They wrote. I turned the flipchart back to the assessment sheet. I asked Mark and Tom to write in their self-rating numbers. Then I wrote my numbers for them. Mine were all zeroes.

| | Mark | Tom | Gus for Mark | Gus for Tom |
|---|---|---|---|---|
| Respect as a person | 3 | 0 | 0 | 0 |
| Support and encouragement | 4 | 1 | 0 | 0 |
| Courage to challenge wrongs | 1 | 7 | 0 | 0 |

"Those are pretty harsh numbers, Gus," said Tom.

"They are, aren't they? A lot of big deltas, big differences. Big gaps."

"You know," said Mark. "We get no slack from you."

"I hear that. It feels bad when I never give you guys a break. I'm sorry that I've been so tough. I'll be more encouraging. It makes me wonder, how much slack do you give each other?"

Tom adjusted his perfect tie. Mark studied his nails.

"Good job on the ratings," I said happily. "That was the easy part."

They groaned. I turned the sheet.

"Like the Courageous Communication Model, the Black Box Solutions Model has four artful steps."

*The Black Box Solutions Model*

1. *Assess* what's broken.
2. *Accept* the failure.
3. *Repair* the failure.
4. *Team up* and work together.

"Let's look at the first step.

## 1. Assess What's Broken

"Let's use your numbers. We can see what's broken: You don't re-spect or support and encourage each other. Not much courage. . . .

"The second step in Black Box is very quick." They brightened. I turned the sheet:

## 2. Accept the Failure

"The second step is to accept the failure. Tom, you dislike Mark and won't work with him. On whose orders are you doing this?"

"Mine," he said.

"Mark?"

"Same for me. It's my call."

"Great! You both just took a huge step for mankind. You both took ownership of your ancient feud. How does that feel?"

"Weird," said Tom.

"A little better," said Mark, watching me turn the sheet.

## 3. Repair the Failure

"The third step is to repair the failure.

"Our objective today is civility. Where do we start?"

"Has to be with respect," said Mark.

"Right. Mark, when we first talked, I asked you to describe your behaviors with your mentor, Sy. Please describe them to Tom."

Mark looked at me. "I always laughed at Sy's jokes."

I smiled, "Sy was a funny guy. Please tell that to your colleague."

Grimacing, Mark turned in Tom's direction. Without a hint of eye contact, he said, "I called him regularly. Asked him for advice. I *listened* to his advice. I saw him socially at least once a month."

"Thanks, Mark," I said.

"Now, Tom, please face Mark and tell him the behaviors you show when you're with your favorite customer."

Tom exhaled loudly; this was tough for him. "All right, I'm early for meetings. Captivated by his thoughts. I presume the best for him. I assume all problems are my fault."

I wrote their behavioral answers on a second flipchart.

| *Mark Shows Respect* | *Tom Shows Respect* |
| --- | --- |
| Humor | Early |
| Regular contact | Captivated |
| Ask for and listen to advice | Presume the best |
| Social contact | Take responsibility for problems |

"You've shown total competence in your behaviors with others. What would happen if you showed them to each other?"

"Damn!" said Tom. "I should've known you'd use this against us!"

"Sounds like a resounding *yes* to me," I said. They fell mute. "Give me a professional reason why you should not do it." I smiled.

"Good. We're at the final step."

## 4. Team Up and Work Together

"You're going to figure this out without me. How are you going to team up to fix the failures in respect, in UPR? Today's objective: be civil.

"I need clear, measurable behaviors. How much time do you want?"

They argued and finally agreed on twenty minutes.

"See you in twenty. Good luck, gentlemen."

I left. Outside were two other company vice-presidents.

"We were afraid," one said to me, "of violence in there."

I grinned. "My methods are really quite peaceable."

"How's it going in there?" asked the other VP. "Is there a chance of a fight? You have no idea how much those guys hate each other."

Later, Tom and Mark emerged from the meeting in conversation. Follow-up meetings consolidated their relational work. They and their divisions stopped fighting each other.

Tom Kenner recently agreed to retire.

## Caveats Regarding the Black Box

This Black Box application was presented with a consultant present. Although each of the tools in this book is designed for use by readers, the use of a skilled consultant should be considered in high-acuity, long-term conflicts until personal and institutional experience with the Black Box technique has been gained.

As with all coaching for skill and competence development, it's best to begin with low-level conflicts and work upward. Of course, no tool should be used as the sole means of addressing situations in which physical violence may result. Courage always works best early.

Courage is the backbone of leadership. It remains the key force and the pivot point around which our other strengths are leveraged, high core values are preserved, and personal and institutional integrity are maintained.

The tools represent methods by which courage can more quickly and effectively emerge as the consciously determinative factor of outcomes.

As long as we have the courage to act according to principles and to persist in their application, great results will eventually follow.

We're now ready to consider building those results as a professional with a career, as a leader of an institution, and as an effective member of a family.

# 13

# USING COURAGEOUS COMMUNICATION FROM THE BOTTOM UP

It's when you know you're licked before you begin,
but you begin anyway and you see it through no
matter what.

—*Harper Lee*

So far we have focused on executive coaching for courage. It's well understood that leadership sets corporate culture, just as the mood of parents defines the character of the home. This explains the heavy emphasis on executive training programs.

But what happens if courageous communication isn't being used by people at the top?

Fortunately, courage is accessible to everyone. It's not the unique province of people who go to special schools, come from highly privileged backgrounds, or receive unique executive coaching. Two stories illustrate how courageous communication can be deployed when senior management hasn't bought in to the need for principled change.

## Action-e-Reaction from Subordinate to Superior

Amy Barton has been a young and highly competent surgical nurse in a major East Coast metropolitan hospital for three years. A quick study and a tireless worker, she's appreciated because she's principled, capable, and humorous and because she blesses the world with a warm and engaging smile.

161

Two years ago, she worked for the first time with one of the region's most senior neurosurgeons. She observed him relieve his internal stress during the operation by insulting one of the nurses. Amy felt a jolt of alarm, which was gradually replaced by low-level anxiety. Before the procedure was finished, the surgeon had also scorched Amy without cause.

"Nurse," he snapped at her, "listen up. If you want to succeed here, I strongly suggest no more daydreaming about soap operas."

In neither case did anyone, from senior R.N.'s and the surgical resident to the anesthesiologist, speak up in protest or defense.

Amy was told that the surgeon was known for arrogance, sarcasm, hostility, and impatience and that she shouldn't take it personally. She tried to forget the incident, but she found herself worrying about the doctor and her own responsibilities.

A month later, she was again in surgery with him. Again he derided her and later called her a name. The next day, Amy Barton raised the issue with the charge nurse.

"It's not smart to confront him," she replied. "Just be nice. The guy's hugely important to the hospital, and he brings in major grant money. You don't stand a chance against him."

In the Courageous Communication program, Amy Barton was the first to raise her hand to describe an actual problem that she's facing.

She described the facts I've just stated. "I'm going to be in surgery with this doctor again next month. I'm serious—I'm ready to call in sick, take a short-notice leave, or change my name."

I thanked her for her candor. I said that I had tried those tactics, without success. "This is a classic challenge with a gap in authority, a continuing problem, and no intervention by senior management. You have a classic opportunity to act courageously."

"Wonderful," said Amy, and everyone laughed.

"That's what's funny about courage," I said. "It *is* wonderful." Smiling, I asked the class, "Given this fact pattern and our shot at wonder, what courageous communication tool would you use first with this physician?"

Most suggested Action-e-Reaction, which has the advantages of indisputable impact feedback and shortness of exchange.

"I like that too. The feelings we experience from someone's behaviors are legitimate, regardless of rank. Before we start brainstorming a solution, let me reframe Action-e-Reaction.

"Because this physician has a habit of disrespect, Amy may have to respectfully repeat it each time the doctor is verbally abusive.

"Amy can also use reflecting back and active listening.

"As we noted, it will take a touch of courage. But it's far easier, less emotionally painful, and more principled to act for what is right than to silently suffer abuse and abet wrong behaviors. Initially, it will take restraint for Amy to speak only for herself. Once she establishes a $CR_1$ relationship with this doctor, she can continue by giving an Action-e-Reaction about how he treats others.

"Questions? None? Let's try out this situation in a role-play."

A physician in the class volunteered to be the surgeon. I played the role of Amy Barton. We said that the classroom space represented a private area of the hallway outside the operating room and that the surgeon had again been verbally abusive to Amy during a just completed operation. The "surgeon" exited into the hallway.

"Doctor," I said brightly, with a smile, "could I have a moment?"

"Well, if it isn't our rookie nurse," he said.

"Doctor, I value the opportunity to have a professional and collegial relationship with you. But when you called me a name during surgery, I felt humiliated."

"Well, it's nice to know you were listening."

I smiled briefly. "Yes, I was. Doctor, I welcome your feedback. I would appreciate it if you shared feedback with me in private."

He made a dismissive gesture. "You are confused. You confuse me with someone who cares."

I took a breath to hear the insult and allow me to remain with the courage to stay in the moment and in the tool.

"Thank you, Doctor. This wasn't easy for me to say, and I very much appreciate your listening to me."

The surgeon shrugged and walked away.

"Now," I said to the class, "Amy has delivered a clear and courageous piece of communication. We probably saw no immediate, dramatic results. Does that mean nothing's changed?"

"She's made a stand for what's right," said one.

"He's on notice that she won't tolerate this silently," said another.

"That's right. Let's imagine that before long, we're in surgery again, and once more he insults me. After surgery, I wait for him, he appears—the role-player returns—and I say this to him:

"Doctor, I value the opportunity to have a professional and collegial relationship with you. But when you called me a name during surgery, I felt humiliated."

"What are you, a parrot looking for a shoulder?"

"Doctor, I welcome all the feedback I can get. I would appreciate it if you would share that feedback with me in private."

"Wow, déjà vu all over again!"

"Yes, it does sound as if we've been here before, doesn't it?"

He looks at her, hoping she'll disappear. Maintaining firm and respectful eye contact, her body square to his larger one, she stands her ground and patiently waits.

"You're not going to go away, are you?"

"No, Doctor, I'm not. I hope you don't either."

The surgeon sighs audibly. "OK, OK, I'm sorry! Now go away."

I complimented the role-player and clapped my hands as everyone else applauded his excellent engagement and his obvious capture of the surgeon's affect.

I asked Amy what she thought of it so far.

"That was realistic, and that's what he's really like, but I'm not sure I could do that twice with him!"

"I hear you. The first time we try these tools, we have anxiety and we have fear. And we may not get the Nobel Prize. We might stumble, blubber. But we can persist. We can face the fear. Amy, if you decide to do this, do you think he'll stop?"

"I think he will," she said.

"I agree. Why not ask the person who was playing the doc?"

Amy asked the role-player, " Will this work with that person?"

He said, "Gus made it very difficult for me to keep arguing with him. Amy, I think if you use that with that surgeon, he will stop his bad acting. It really takes away his sense of power."

Amy then agreed to do the role-play herself.

She engaged the surgeon with a courageously respectful Action-e-Reaction. Knowing the situation so well, she did far better than I did.

Amy felt equipped, and she resolved to address the surgeon, leaving the program with her trademark smile. We later learned that Amy had succeeded in encouraging the physician to stop verbally abusing nurses.

## Looking for What's Right

A second example about using courageous communication from the bottom up comes to us from a national business law firm that I'll call Bodenheimer, Hogan, Dykstra, and King, or BDHK.

In the 1980s, after a series of New York mergers, BDHK launched a new focus on making money. After initial savings and major profit-taking by senior partners, the firm was hit by client management challenges, loss of clients, merger complications, turnover, schisms, divisiveness, triangulation, credit theft, gossip, abuse, and bad acting. In short, BDHK lost momentum and some of its top people, but there was no diminution in the drive for profits.

Adrienne Helms, a BDHK senior partner, heard me speak about courage at a bar function and suggested a business lunch. She was affable, relational, and very clear.

"We look like one firm," she said to me over terrific *dim-sum*, "but in reality, we're divided into the original three major premerger law offices, each with its own way of doing things. The groups don't talk. Worse, they compete, and lawyers from DEF, the rival firm we absorbed last year, are at war with the veteran BDHK folks. Even the senior partners have issues. We lack the good things—leadership, teamwork, support, professionalism.

"We're losing our productivity to friction and politics. We're starting to lose our most promising associates. You work in this kind of environment. Can we interest you?"

"I am if the senior partners are interested. I'm less so if they're not. How interested are they?"

"They're not. But I am. I liked your talk. Why don't you show me your consulting stuff and I'll take it back to them."

I nodded. "OK. What were BDHK's core values—actual operating principles—before the first merger?" I explained core values.

"Professionalism and integrity," said Adrienne.

"What are they now?"

"We're now a business," said Adrienne. "We focus on profits, productivity, and efficiency. Law is a great deal more competitive than it was thirty years ago. We have to run by the bottom line."

"The pressure to make money is incredible," I said.

"But I didn't hear you use that as a driver in your talk."

"I didn't. Making money's not a high core value; it's produced by high core values. Let me ask you: when the firm's at its best, what are the actual core values that are at work?"

"We're supposed to do three things," she said. "Know our stuff, carry our load, and get along." She thought for a moment. "Those aren't high core values, are they? They're medium core values. So our clever motto represents, let's see, competence, accountability, and cooperation. But the high ones are different. They're integrity, courage, and character."

"The ethicists of the world need you among their ranks," I said. "What if you extrapolated that the only reason I'm here is to make as much money off of you as I can?"

She sat back. "I'd understand it, but I wouldn't like it."

"Right! Understandable but not admirable. Now imagine that you meet my older sister. She knows as much as I do, but she has a reputation for seeking right outcomes, of being extremely trustworthy and totally principled. In other words, she's not driven by profit."

"Obviously, I'd want her," said Adrienne.

"So would I! So how does BDHK conceal its core value of profit-seeking from its clients, staff, courts, law schools, and new hires?

"I have to say that I see your negative organizational frictions and interpersonal dynamics as totally predictable. They track back to your wanting to optimize profit instead of maximizing principles. I think it's what happens when advocates of justice become profit sharks."

I then answered her hard questions about Courageous Communication programs. I thanked her for lunch, and we shook hands and said good-bye.

Months later, Adrienne Helms phoned. "The partners don't want the program, but they recognize that their department chiefs, admin managers, and senior administrators need it. Some of our nonmanaging lawyers need it. Would you be willing to train them first?"

"I might. Why won't the partners take the program?"

"I was supposed to tell you that they couldn't get their calendars to agree, but I actually think it's because they're not ready to change."

"I'll do it if the partners promise to keep an open mind about taking the program themselves."

They promised. I taught the program. Near the end of the program, I asked the participants to present actual communication dilemmas for us to consider.

"Here are the rules of the road," I said. "When the fact pattern suggests a person by name, we never mention the name. We hold the situation in confidence. We show respect to those not present. Questions or problems with that?" There were none.

"I have a problem for you," said senior attorney Ryan "Murph" Murphy. "I have to work with a senior associate who was with DEF. We used to do cases against each other. Now, whenever we end up on the same litigation team, he ignores my presence until he criticizes my methods, as if I were a first-year associate. The problem is that BDHK taught me my methods, and I've been a litigator for fifteen years.

"They had a different culture at DEF, and they're holding on to it as stubbornly, I guess, as we are to ours." He paused and looked at his new colleagues from other firms. "Now, I've spoken to him directly, one on one, and he looks at me the way snakes look at mice.

"I took the issue to the managing partner. She said that she'd seen this dynamic in the past and that we'd just have to ride these personality conflicts out, sort of like waiting out the flu.

"The problem is that this is more like a chronic disease. But I honestly believe that if I use reflecting back or Action-e-Reaction, I'll get push-back from him and a worsening situation."

People nod around the room. "Are you nodding," I asked, "because you know of this situation or because this situation is being repeated throughout the firm?"

"It's epidemic," said one. Others agreed.

"Thank you, Ryan. A classic fact pattern with two people of unequal rank, a long-term issue, and no senior management intervention available, and it represents a systemic challenge."

On the board, I wrote the words, *moral imperative*. "The concept of moral imperative invites us to look for what's right in the fog of conflict. Moral imperative means cutting to the ultimate chase." Let's climb up to 1,200 feet, where we can see ten miles even with clouds, and do grand thinking on this situation.

"Ryan, the associate has bad feelings about you. We have people from three mergers in this room, and everyone knows this general situation. Respectfully, let's name those feelings."

More than one said, "Arrogance." I wrote that on the flipchart.

"Anger." "Pride." "Loathing." "Meanness."

As the words came, some people sat straighter. A few smiled and nodded with the freedom of lending reality a name.

"A pretty list," I said. "These feelings produce what behaviors in him?"

"He ignores me, then criticizes me," said Murph.

"That's right. First disdain, then insults."

I wrote down the words. "Now, let's use our high-end analytical skills. What do you think causes him to feel these things around Ryan?"

A long silence. Ryan said, "I guess he's angry about the merger. His partnership candidacy and ownership position were reduced. He's not as comfortable as he used to be. Maybe I represent that loss to him."

"Excellent. Comments?"

Others said that Ryan's analysis was correct.

I said, "We have a senior associate who's suffered disappointment over things he couldn't control. He's angry. We see him tightening up on things he can influence, such as litigation protocol and how he treats other people.

"Ryan, can we look at your situation?" He nodded. "What behaviors do you demonstrate to this senior associate?"

Ryan grimaced and pulled on an ear. "I react badly to him. I'm curt. Not very respectful myself. Defensive. Resentful."

"Murph, you've walked out on him," said one. Ryan agreed. Others chimed in. I wrote, "Curt. Disrespectful. Defensive. Inattentive. Interruptive," on the other flipchart.

"In considering moral imperatives, we look for the principles, the largest and deepest values available to critical thinking. How do we insert high principles into Murph's relationship with this associate?"

"I have to demonstrate high principles even if he doesn't," said Murph. "I can't let another person rob me of my integrity and lower my behaviors to the point that they match his."

"Well captured, counselor," I said. "Otherwise, we're walking around our offices with a giant sandwich board that says, I'LL LOWER MY STANDARDS IF YOU LOWER YOURS.

"So," continued Murph, "I have to recognize that this guy is feeling bad and defensive, and my jamming my majority methods on him is not helping his ability to cope."

"Can you compromise on litigation protocols?" I asked. I reminded them that the ethicist Stephen L. Carter teaches us that compromise that advances integrity is good and that compromise that retards integrity is not.

"Sure I can. I wouldn't do it for him and his arrogant ways. But I can do it for principle."

"Why not do it for him out of UPR, unconditional positive respect?" I asked.

"Hmm, you got me," he said.

We set up a role-play. Murph, who knew the senior associate's behaviors as well as anyone in the room, played his own antagonist, whom we named Henry Cardozo. I played the role of the injured Murph.

I thought, *I'm going to need UPR and the Courageous Communication Model. I may have to use reflecting back, Action-e-Reaction, Black Box, and the moral imperative. I might have to use a fire extinguisher.*

Even though it was a role-play in my area of practice, I felt that familiar zing of cortisol as I prepared to listen and to deal with anger.

"Henry Cardozo," I said warmly, "how are you?" I was opening on collegiality, speaking to a comrade instead of to a sworn enemy.

"Mumph," said Cardozo.

*More collegiality. Remember,* I said to myself, *be ethical, supportive, encouraging.*

"I want our work to go well," I said.

Cardozo angrily pushed back from his desk. "You want it to go well?" he repeated, sarcastically using an echo-back. "Then look around! Realize that your procedures make no sense and that you're making a shambles of our ability to work!"

"I can see I've upset you," I said, listening and empathizing.

Henry Cardozo's eyeballs shifted, looking for words. He was ready to fight, to swing away, but in this moment, he could find no opponent, no threat, no target to strike.

*Ask questions.* "What can I do to be of help and not a hindrance?"

"OK," he said, "change your procedures. Rewrite these sections!" He opened an imaginary file and pointed at many pages.

"In the style of the old DEF firm?" I asked. *More questions to understand so I can repair the relationship.*

"Yes!" said Cardozo.

"OK!" I said enthusiastically.

"That's it? You're agreeing?"

"Absolutely," I said. "I may get in trouble with the powers that be, but I'll take the hit. I want to be your colleague."

"And what if I ask you to cut some corners?"

"Then I'll still be your colleague. Nothing can shake my respect for you. But I won't cut the corners. Let's get to work."

Henry Cardozo sat in semishock. "You make it impossible to fight you. To stay angry at you."

"It's not me," I said. "It's the behaviors of courage."

We applauded Murph for playing his nemesis.

"What does this exercise teach us?" I asked.

I wrote down their responses:

1. Anyone can use courageous communication.

2. Acting courageously doesn't require senior management agreement.

3. Courage begins as an individual competence.

We then analyzed and role-played solutions to other challenging relationships. Murph and the others resolved to deploy the behaviors of courage in their professional situations.

I have taught many subjects, from Chinese history and creative writing to trial tactics and boxing. For decades, I have attentively watched adult learners exit classrooms. I've seen them leave with a light heart and a tired step, with a sense of hope and a stooped back, with the uplift of resolve and the gravity of despair. Nothing, however, has produced the lightheartedness, the sense of hope, and the inspiration of resolve as the subject of courage.

# Part Three

# GROWING YOUR COURAGE

American public opinion has focused on the link between people's private lives and their public personas. Is it fair to hold people to the same standards at home as at work? How do we feel about execs that make money for us but cheat customers and their families?

Courage is a universal principle and the central competence of character. It's the steel backbone of leadership and the quality that separates great from good. On the other hand, it's not a packet of catsup that we can squeeze onto our character plates at will.

Courage is developed in life, as opposed to cubicles or living rooms. In Chapter Three, we explored courage, integrity, and character. These qualities describe a whole and integrated person who consistently demonstrates principled conduct under stress. This requires practice.

In Part Three, we will see how the tools we've examined apply to our personal lives.

Courage, integrity, character, and leadership require personal change. When you grow these, you are equipped to provide sustainable benefits to everyone around you.

# Part Three

# GROWING YOUR COURAGE

# 14

# EVERYDAY HABITS
# THAT BUILD COURAGE

Gloucester, 'tis true that we are in great danger; the
greater therefore should our courage be.
                    —*William Shakespeare*, Henry V

The lad froze, large eyes popping, pupils widening. He was only five,
but adrenaline was probably making his little mouth very dry.

The man's angry shouts had made the boy flinch. His *Sesame
Street* friends—stuffed figures of Elmo and Big Bird—smiled as they
always did, but they no longer seemed happy.

The man didn't see that, not then. He only remembered them
later, the small, silent, furry witnesses to unhappiness. The man focused on the number of toys strewn across the room, the sheer vol-
ume of them, the ridiculous expanse of them, and none of them
picked up despite a clear instruction to the boy to do so. No one in
the history of Matchbox cars and light sabers and Etch-a-Sketches
had owned so many toys, and they were all here. It had been one of
those days—no, one of those *years*. The man was often angry and
always heatedly denied it. He no longer slept well, had hyperten-
sion, was gaining weight, and was spending more time earning
money and fighting for power than being with his family.

He curbed his frustrations at the office and managed anger on
the flights and the daily commute, only to return from one of his
three regional offices to find this mess.

*All the kid had to do was pick up the darn toys.*

The man tried to not see the fear in his son's eyes, the tears, the
hurt. He knew it was caused by his yelling, but he couldn't stop.

Another moment of looking might touch something within him, so he looked away.

What he saw chilled his hardening heart.

His wife and daughter were transfixed at the door, looking at him, paralyzed by the echoes of his angry words. He saw the fear in their eyes. Suddenly he was no longer a middle-aged man with labor issues, executive responsibilities, revenue stress, and federal safety laws.

He was again a lad of five. His father was shouting and scaring him to his bones, the roar of the angry voice melting marrow and will. Older sisters turned away as the violence began. The man had fulfilled his worst fear: *he had become his own father.*

The man did what bullies do when they're caught in the act of torment: run, hide, and immediately blame others.

Uncomfortably, he left the room.

## Coaching for Courage

Later, finding remnants of courage, he apologized to his wife and daughter. His wife coached him by asking what skills might be missing in his parenting inventory.

"I focus on results," he said. "I don't seem to have any empathy."

She reminded him of his training, of what he taught others. Couldn't that help at home? He knew it could, though he feared to face himself and the pain of the past. His heart slugging, he went to his son's room and sat on the floor, close to him.

"Son, when you didn't pick up your toys, I felt angry." It was a clear and solid Action-e-Reaction statement.

"Sorry, Daddy," said the boy.

The man frowned; maybe these tools don't work in families. Maybe not with youngsters. He then tried the four-step Courageous Communication Model: *Collegial communication. Listening actively with Empathy. Asking questions on point. Relating respectfully.* The heavy lifters of principled speech.

"I want to be a better dad to you," he said warmly. "You had to be pretty scared when I yelled at you. I'm sorry about that." The man was trying to express empathy and show respect by asking questions.

The boy nodded.

"I am sorry, Son," said the man. "I hope you can forgive me."

"I forgive you, Daddy," said the boy quickly, smiling and hugging his dad. The father thanked his son, and he cried a little as he hugged him, losing his voice, and using the hug as the collegiality coda to the model.

Like all of us, he had carefully toted into adulthood the communication patterns he had learned as a kid. As he had once feared his angry parents, now his son feared him. As the man had once helplessly trembled under his father's rage, he now trembled, almost helplessly, with his own internal storms. By denying fear, he was mastered by fear.

He realized that he was at the river and his greatest Point of Decision. Jobs change and careers shift, but his relationship with his son would echo onward for generations. It was the one job in his life he could not morally transfer to anyone else.

What was he carrying into his Point of Decision—courage, integrity, and character? No. His true core values were judgment, anger, and a demand for results. Those would fail at work, and he was using them with his son.

To act rightly, he'd need to cleave to his highest core values. He shook his head; he'd have to totally redesign his operating principles, his system of beliefs. So he intentionally sought the courage to change, which became easier once he experienced the stark and naked humility that comes from seeing the need to rebuild everything.

## Courage Changed Everything

Seeking courage changed everything. I was the crippled man, and the precious lad was my son, Eric. I had grown up watching heroes on the screen. Now I tried to not become the villain of my own family.

The result was that I changed who I was; I practiced new relational habits. I kept at them even while drowning in the incompetence that comes with initial learning. Once I had boxed when I thought I couldn't and jumped out of airplanes I was sure would kill me. Too embarrassed to quit, I just stayed with it.

It meant that the energy that I once spent on chasing money and politics went first to changing myself and then, in greater measure, to serving my family and others.

Today, our adult children are strong, confident and principled. They possess a life ethic and a power of integrity that I could not even imagine when I was their age. They are brave and happy, showing the power of courage to surpass our greatest weaknesses. For years, I apologized to my son, who never failed to forgive me.

I tell this story because courage is not like committee meetings, a thing to be experienced only at work. I tell it because, try as we might to be separate personas, we're the same character in the office and at the dinner table. I could act nicely either way, but I fooled no one. Character leaks out until it becomes an irresistible flood.

I could not be an effective leader while being a defective member of a family; I could not truly honor, encourage, and support all persons at work if I were an emotionally squawking Donald Duck at home.

A few of us have the strength of character to ditch bad habits like changing a flat. Some only change for a catastrophic life-altering event. Others modify conduct out of shame—a Damascene road event that reveals the unacceptability of old habits. Some change because of the generosity of others in the form of mentoring, coaching, and support.

Others will rely on intellect in encountering a person, a story, a program, a book, a CD that inspires discernment and the desire to be decisively different. A few of us, like me, require the entire plethora of all possible inroads into our stubbornness. Many will decide to not change at all.

Confucius said that discernment is the best path to wisdom, and experience, the most bitter. Character, said Thomas Paine, is much easier kept than recovered. But however we get there, get there we must.

In my experience working with fifty industries, the straightest road to courage and change is . . . affection. When we own the discipline of respecting others, we can't help it—we end up caring for them.

When that happens, we are ready to cross the river for them, for principle. It begins with accepting how relational we truly are. Great teams, whether in the military, business, sports, or life, build on that truth. Dysfunctional, fractionated, and divisive groups deny it. No caring, no teamwork.

That is why the theme to our programs is this:

Learn    Do    Be

First we *learn*. Then we *practice*. Only then do we *become*.

When we practice the behaviors of listening, we hear clearly.

When we practice the behaviors of respect, we care truly.

When we practice the behaviors of courage, we become courageous. When we practice the behaviors of courageous leadership, we lead powerfully. Then, when others learn and practice, we collectively become an admirable community. This is the irresistible power of the courageous and principled relationship, $CR_1$.

## Developing Insight

Few people thought that John Daniel, the future president of a U.S. multinational technology firm, lacked insight. This robustly confident senior executive, large and full of presence, had performed brilliantly at Oxford, been raised inside the company as an expatriate with an English accent, was named a senior VP of the European division when he was thirty-eight, and has a family that has adjusted to his corporate demands.

Like most people at his level, he is gifted in intellect, education, ambition, and speech. He has a strong personal presence, a bad back, and a voice that might have drawn a smile from the great Paul Robeson.

In our first executive coaching cycle, John got his FIRO-B results. The *Fundamental Interpersonal Relations Orientation-Behavior* instrument was designed by William Schutz in the 1950s to measure human preferences in relationships. It showed that John Daniel dramatically preferred control over the more relational factors of inclusion and affection. The scores suggested a dictator.

"OK, but I'm a *benevolent* dictator. I care for my people."

He then learned from a 360-degree assessment from his direct reports and peers that he was intimidating his people. He shook his head sadly.

"Absolutely, I had no concept of that."

Most of us overrate our own abilities.[1] When one finds oneself being rated much lower by others, there is a deep and natural emotional letdown.

I reminded him that the assessment was about perception and not reality. That the 360-degree report provided calibrated feedback to empower him. With it, he could make any behavioral changes he wished.

"Imagine," I suggested, "how well things will work when you're no longer seen as intimidating."

He reflected on that. Change, like courage, sinks deep into our DNA.

"How would you feel if your people gave you strong, assertive, and candid opinions that ran counter to your own views?"

"I'd love to get honest feedback from them in daily conversation. But I never do." A pause. "*Aha*. They don't because they're intimidated. Honestly, do I seem intimidating? I know I was shopping at Euro Big and Tall's when in grade school, but I am as friendly a man as you'll know."

After further thought, John added, "I can really be salty, but I thought that my people were immune. That they knew I mean no harm."

"Is it possible that some of them don't know that?"

He nodded.

We rehearsed the Black Box for two difficult situations that he faced at work. After flying home, he started using courageous communication in many different office situations. John reported back, first by e-mail and then by phone, that the results were good but not great.

"Why less than great?" I asked. It was a really clear connection; he sounded as if he were next door.

"It seems I have a problem with my wife."

He said he comes home in such a foul mood that all he can do is mindlessly watch Eurosport and BBC and "some despicable French programs."

He's too worn out to focus on the communication model and the bleeding Action-e-Reaction and the beastly three acts of courageous leadership.

When his wife, Alison, asked him—before he flew to America to meet with me—if he'd help her with dinner, he replied, "Do it yourself, dear."

She cried. He yelled. That worked so well, particularly with his brick-shattering voice, that she's permitted him to sleep on the sofa ever since.

"My back hurts. It kills, really."

I asked him to name the behaviors that Alison hated most.

Coming home tired and unpleasant

Not hugging the child or asking about her day

Going directly into the parlor and turning on the television

Giving orders (consistent with his high FIRO-B control score) about how to make dinner, clean the house, and pick up toys (inside, I groaned)

Arguing (360-degree feedback said he was intimidating), which inspires bad feelings, tears, and the opportunity to sleep much closer to the primary television

I wrote them down and thanked him for his candor and courage. "What's your goal, John?"

"My goal? My goal is to recover my wife's love and our marriage. What an idiot I am! Nothing else counts."

"This was obviously happening when you were in the U.S. for coaching. What kept you from raising then the most important issue in your life?"

"I'm not sure. No—not true. I was too embarrassed. Isn't that a lark? I didn't know you; you're not truly part of my world. Your opinion of me, good or bad, wouldn't exactly alter the earth's rotation, and I spent hours posing for you as if Euro world sales depended on my pitch."

"A very human reaction."

"But not very top-drawer. Not very presidential."

"OK. You're not performing at the desired level. What stops you from changing your behaviors right now?"

"Good question. I'm not sure. I feel a curious paralysis."

"Maybe there are too many behaviors to change at once?"

"Yes, that's part of it."

"Sometimes, John, we're afraid to try change because we're afraid we won't be able to pull it off."

There was a long silence. "That's also part of it."

"We can also fear that we'll make things worse."

"Not sure that's possible. But I'm writing these down."

"We often worry that in trying to change, we'll look like idiots."

"That, on the other hand, is most *definitely* possible."

"When we're afraid to intervene or approach conflict—"

"And I don't like conflict," he tossed in.

"You're in the majority of millions with that. John, when we shy away from solving conflicts at work, what's our deepest fear? Our catastrophic expectation?"

"That they'll rip off my tunic and fire me and my broken ways."

I asked him how realistic that fear was.

He said not very realistic.

"What's your catastrophic fear with Alison?"

The silence was painful. Finally, his voice choked.

"I'm afraid she'll leave me. Take our daughter and leave me."

"How realistic is that fear?"

On the phone, he wrestled with that fear, trying to find a place to run, to escape. He was at the river. I heard him breathing as if running. Now he would either show backbone or go slackbone. He faced it.

"Not very likely," he said.

"I'm very proud of you! You faced your fear! You've seen how it can stop us only because we overrate its power. Now, is it possible that if you don't try to change your behaviors, she'll think you don't love her and your daughter enough to make the attempt?"

"Hmm. That I value my fear over her?"

Paradoxically, we suffer far more when we let fear stop us than when we face it and boldly move forward. Our fears are overrated. We create Goliaths out of gnats and jump because of shadows on our feelings. We flinch at emotions instead of boldly running at the real problems that the feelings heralded for us. We avoid issues instead of boldly seeking solutions until the problem is fixed. We do this first, in ourselves. Second, in our families. Third, in our other work.

I challenged John to change one behavior. "Pick one," I said.

"Which? The easiest? Most difficult? The one that bothers Alison the most? That one that drives our girl barmy?"

I sent a smile across the Atlantic. "What counts is that you intend to change—the commitment to no longer accept the painful results of avoidance. John, once you *intend*, you can pick anything."

He chose the telly; he would no longer hide in a video box.

John had begun the discipline of changing his everyday habits. He was consciously—and uncomfortably—replacing behaviors so that they enriched his relationships instead of destroying them.

He thought it was not unlike learning your first foreign language after being strictly monolingual or learning to eat with your opposite hand. At first, it's awkward. Later, it's no big deal.

- It required a commitment to everyday practice of the new behavior.

- It required the ability to ask for forgiveness when he inadvertently returned to old habits.
- It required behavioral courage at home as a high core value. It required some accountability—in this case, to his family and to a lesser degree to his coach.

This conversation took place two autumns ago. By Christmas, John—a brilliant, fast learner—had changed his controlling others into serving them. He had converted an entitled sense of self-absorption into consciously enjoying the pleasure of others, bullying into collegiality, and intimidation into a graceful and affirmative presence.

By using the behavioral skills in the Courageous Communication Model, in Action-e-Reaction, and the three acts of courageous leadership with his wife and daughter, John allowed himself to grow his courage while modeling principled behaviors for his family. Let's not be shy about this: we're looking at happiness.

John reports that his marriage has been resurrected; that he is in love with Alison and his daughter. He also says that work is a pleasure.

This is not astonishing. What's astonishing is that so few of us will look at the amount of friction in our lives and not make changes.

In the next chapter, we'll explore a personal accountability tool that will let you assess your courage and your character. Don't think of it as a visit to the doctor's office in which bad news potentially looms. Think of it instead as a visit to a character spa where the concepts refresh, the practice builds strength, and the waters heal the scars of bad habits.

Realize that in the midst of a busy life, you are now afforded a rare and special opportunity to learn the most important facts about yourself.

Visualize that you are about to experience a private, one-on-one meeting with Moses, Confucius, and Aristotle and that it'll remain confidential between the four of you, making it appropriate for you to build your most important strength.

# 15

# YOUR CHARACTER QUOTIENT

I always wanted to be somebody, but I should have
been more specific.

—*Lily Tomlin*

In an old English legend, whoever could pull a great sword from a
massive stone would immediately be named the next king of En-
gland. The test was not about the abdominal core; it was about high
core values, about strength of character and heart.

The strongest knights of the realm eagerly—and avariciously—
tried to wrench the blade free. All failed until a young farm boy named
Arthur, who needed to immediately find a tournament sword for his
older brother, saw the deeply imbedded sword and quickly drew it from
the rock. In instinctively serving others—his brother and family—
Arthur demonstrated principled behavior and selflessness.

## The Modern Character Stone

But without a modern-day character stone, how might we assess our
own competencies of courage and character?

Aristotle and Churchill would say that this is the most important knowledge you can obtain about yourself. It's more important
than knowing if you're popular, perceived as skilled, or thought of
as having good hair (or any hair at all).

Individually, knowing your Character Quotient identifies your
areas of strength and helps you become one of Jim Collins's right

people to get on the bus.[1] Tactically, it helps you develop and practice the courageous behaviors that produce business excellence and Aristotelian happiness. Strategically, it aligns your conduct and your team's operations and family life with high core values and sustainable success. Big words, clear path.

The Character Quotient has a very different purpose than the Black Box. The Black Box is used when there has been a serious crash in relationships. The Character Quotient is a tool for personal measurement of our character separate from a high-end conflict situation.

I found it useful to first break courage and character into three categories and then to define each category in measurable behaviors. I was doing this work when I got a phone call from Chuck Pappalardo.

Chuck is managing director of Trilogy Venture Search, an executive headhunting firm that serves Fortune 100 clients. Chuck grew up with five siblings in a tightly knit working-class neighborhood on the east side of Cleveland. There were so many adults that shared high core values that mistrust and thuggery weren't permitted. It was the kind of place where parents looked out for each other's families. This meant that kids could get away with *nothing*. It also meant that everything, from family integrity and recipes to community responsibility and childhood colds, was shared.

Chuck's dad ran a small business forms firm and was the only member of his original family to graduate from high school. Chuck's mom was a champion Tupperware salesperson who won awards, cars, dining room sets, and minibikes. Chuck recalls Amish customers who paid for products with live chickens. Most important was that she loved her family, her neighbors, newcomers on the street, and strangers in the world.

Both parents specialized in teaching their kids to take responsibility, to admit when you're wrong, and to take care of other people. His mother emphasized manners and politeness. The family had dinner together every night. Cross-talking wasn't permitted, and no one left the table until the adults were done exploring all the issues of the day. Early on, Chuck became a good listener.

Chuck was six when he played too rough with another kid. Mr. Pappalardo made Chuck go to the kid's family and apologize, because his dad had high core values and was focused on imparting them to the kids. The father's brother Joe, a blue-collar worker at Pabst Blue Ribbon and Ohio Rubber, was cut from the same cloth.

Uncle Joe's schooling had ended in the ninth grade, but he continued his learning as an Army machine gunner in World War II and as a person who always stood up for the underdog in every factory in which he worked. Chuck remembers his mom, his dad, and Uncle Joe doing the right thing, again and again, without fail.

Whether it was spending time on a momentarily wayward kid, helping a neighbor in crisis, sharing measles so all the kids on the street could get it over with, or standing up in the shop for a worker who was being mistreated, these three adults imprinted courageous living, respectful relating, and principled labor into the deep character development circuits of the youth around them.

As a result, when Chuck saw unethical practices in his own career path, he didn't look the other way, cross the street, or suddenly check the time. He intuitively discerned right from wrong, boldly acted for what is right regardless of risk to himself, and moved forward despite fear and trepidation to ensure that there would be no repetition of the injustice against someone else. This made him a substantial executive and an admirable adult; consistent with ancient wisdom, it also made him happy.

"I hear you're an ethicist," Chuck Pappalardo said with what I think of as an inner-city accent—direct, candid, lyrical, and engaging.

"Yes, despite my feet of clay," I said.

"And every year you give an integrity talk at West Point?"

"I do, even though the participants often riot."

He laughed. "I want to know how I can measure my own ethics. I'm trying to understand how to help employers recruit ethical execs. I think I have a better than average understanding of ethics, but I'm the first to admit that I don't have the vocabulary. I don't know how to name what I need to measure. Here's the deal—employers won't talk about a person's ethics because they're afraid of legal liability. I want you to tell me how to do it."

"That's a great request. Let me ask you: does 'ethics' mean to you principled conduct, integrity, and courage under pressure?"

"Yes, it does."

"*Ethics* is following an ethical code. So if the code's weak in content or enforcement, a so-called ethical person could be useless in a moral crisis. I think what we really want is the courage to act rightly."

"OK. I never thought of it that way, but I agree."

I asked, "Do you think courage can be described in behaviors?"

He thought. "I think I know what courage looks like."

I asked for his e-mail address and immediately sent him an attachment. "I'm sending an integrity glossary. I wonder if you'd be willing to read it and then tell me your thoughts."

"I got it," he said a second later. "I'm reading."

| The Integrity Glossary | |
| --- | --- |
| Good Person | Person of Character |
| Honesty (truth) | Integrity (acting for what is right) |
| Honor (no lying, cheating, or stealing) | Courage (stopping wrongs) |
| Ethics (following ethical rules) | Character (sustained integrity and courage) |

"Let me get this straight," said Chuck. "The good person is just that—someone who keeps his or her nose clean. But I see it—the person of character is a completely different cat; this person does the right thing not only for himself or herself but for others. For the principle of a thing. I grew up with people like that."

"See, you're an ethicist, too. More accurately, you're a *couragist*. Just as there's a huge gap between a *good person* and a *person of character*, there's an equivalently huge gap between ethics and courage."

"OK, Gus. But everyone doesn't have your glossary. At least not yet. See, some of my clients say that right and wrong's relative. Some think that no one's really wrong and no one person can say what's right."

"I hear that too. What's interesting is that a group of super-talented researchers, led by Robert House, a Wharton biz prof, did some great international research on this. They found that across world cultures, *all people* admire the same leadership qualities of respect and trustworthiness.[2]

"OK," he said. "If I wanted to assess my own level of courage, as you put it, how would I do it?"

"To measure your own moral, relational, and personal courage, you could assess your ability to take the moral hills that crop up every day in business and in life."

"I like that. Keep going."

"I assess courage competencies in three buckets. I call it the Courage Quotient. Churchill called courage the first of all human qualities, the one that guarantees all the others. If you want to be respectful, it takes courage to make sure you actually honor all others.

"When you use it, you develop a map of your own character strengths and challenges that can lead to a coherent plan for development."

Chuck asked more questions. He was thorough. I used to be a prosecutor, but I felt like a chew toy being tested by a canine consumer agency. I was mentally flipped, impact-measured, distance-thrown, and shaken side to side with some gut-check growls thrown in.

"OK," he said, "I like it. I want you to send me the Character Quotient. This is a first step toward discovering how this company can help our clients hire people of courage, of character."

I said, "But you have to promise to use this special power only for the good of the planet and, more specifically, only to align your operations with the highest core values."

He said he would, and he has.

The Character Quotient further equips our development of courageous behaviors.

Executives like Chuck and those he places have to inspire others to their best selves every day, day after day. They have to model how to relate according to principle instead of by mood or fear or pressure. They do this when they make performance not about themselves but about high values. That decision takes guts. This is a rare quality because we are not intentional about building the competence of courage.

Leading is about others, but leading effectively depends on one thing more than any other: the leader's courage. The leader's courage under stress will emerge in his or her actions, words, decisions, and physical presence.

Thus authentic and effective leadership education begins with candid self-assessment. Assessment reveals strengths and challenges and highlights the internal changes required to improve the capacity to act for what is right and to correct wrongs.

Assessing our courage and our character is more important than gauging our economic, physical, and emotional health. Why? Because all other indicators are dependent on our "first human quality."

The Character Quotient is a means by which we can calibrate feedback on our courage and effectively equip us to act according to principle.

We once required high-integrity families, such as Chuck Pappalardo's, to develop our character. That's no longer available to everyone. Now it can be undertaken by self-assessment and practice.

For the tool to work, the person taking it has to be candid. It's a private and confidential self-evaluation tool that invites us to trust ourselves. This is not so easy.

Please prepare to be brutally honest about yourself.

## The Character Quotient (CQ)

The Character Quotient is an individual discernment tool. It should never be used by an organization to assess for personnel actions.

The CQ has three measurable scales to gauge your behavioral development as a courageous leader:

A. Deep concerns
B. Their impact on my behaviors and those of others
C. Courageous objectives

First, you ask yourself about your true, deep concerns (A):

What is providing the greatest pressure deep within me? This is something that we normally hide from all others. It's almost always a fear.

Only you (and perhaps your executive coach) will see this answer. You can afford to be honest. The wisdom is within you.

Then you ask, what is the impact of those pressures on my actions (B)?

How do those pressures show up in my behaviors?

This step, like anything important, requires solid reflection. Take your time. Inventory your less than perfect behaviors. Ask for candid feedback on your behaviors from those courageous enough to provide it. (If you receive little feedback, the best way to improve that is to provide encouragement, support, and mostly positive feedback to others.) And don't question, argue with, or punish anyone for the feedback.

Lastly, you identify your courageous behavioral objectives—the new behaviors you want (C):

Which are my least courageous behaviors, and which courageous behaviors do I intend to develop in their place?

Please complete the Character Quotient alone. Allow yourself sixty uninterrupted minutes. An hour to candidly assess your competence in the first human quality is a *de minimus* investment, and it's far more enjoyable than getting a root canal or spending a month answering depositions related to corporate misconduct. Remember that these answers affect everyone in your life.

Keep this document in a safe, secure, and private place.

A.  Deep Concerns

1.  Imagine that someone whom you trust tells you a deep, dark secret. You feel great empathy. It also reminds you of what deeply concerns you, secretly, about yourself. Write that concern here:

    _____
    _____
    _____
    _____

2.  Imagine that you've been working on tough issues. You awake a number of times with those issues pressing on you. Name the issues:

    _____
    _____
    _____
    _____

3.  If you looked deep within your private self, where only you can see, what pressures do you find working on you?

    _____
    _____
    _____
    _____

4.  We all have fears. In that same deep and private place, candidly look at your fears and anxieties. Name them.

    _____
    _____
    _____
    _____

5.  Review your answers to the first four questions. Summarize them in three or four words.

    _____
    _____

B.  Their Impact on My Behaviors and Those of Others

Now that you have named your issues and fears, you will ask yourself the following questions

- What is the impact of these fears on my behaviors?
- What is its impact on my habits?
- What is its impact on my primary relationships at work and home?
- How does it affect my work?
- How does it affect my family?
- How does it affect my health?

6.  Look at your answers to Question 5. How do these deeply held concerns and fears surface in your (a) daily behaviors, (b) habits, (c) relationships, (d) work, (e) family, and (f) health?

(a) _____

_____

_____

(b) _____

_____

_____

(c) _____

_____

_____

(d) _____

_____

_____

(e) _____

_____

_____

(f) _____

_____

_____

C. Courageous Objectives

Now answer this question: What new behavior would I want to replace each fear that I've named?

7. Look at your answers to Question 6. Which three behaviors are the least courageous? To which new behaviors will you change them? (Don't select more than three at a time.)

|                                    |                                                   |
| ---------------------------------- | ------------------------------------------------- |
| *My Least Courageous Behaviors*    | *Will Change to These New Courageous Behaviors*   |

(a) _____         _____

(b) _____         _____

(c) _____         _____

## Follow-Up Step One

Take your answers from the CQ and use them to fill out your chart of Concerns, Impacts, and Objectives (see Figure 15.1). A sample is provided in Figure 15.2.

## Follow-Up Step Two

Use your answers from Section C (Courageous Objectives) to complete your chart of Old Behaviors, New Behaviors, and Accountabilities (see Figure 15.3). A sample is provided in Figure 15.4.

# Figure 15.1. My Concerns, Impacts, and Objectives

Impacts

| Concerns and Fears | Behavior | Habits | Relationships | Work | Family | Health | New Courageous Objectives |
|---|---|---|---|---|---|---|---|
| | | | | | | | |
| | | | | | | | |
| | | | | | | | |
| | | | | | | | |
| Anxieties | | | | | | | |
| | | | | | | | |
| | | | | | | | |
| Concerns | | | | | | | |
| | | | | | | | |
| | | | | | | | |
| | | | | | | | |

# Figure 15.2. Sample Chart of Concerns, Impacts, and Objectives

## Impacts

| Concerns and Fears | Behavior | Habits | Relationships | Work | Family | Health | New Courageous Objectives |
|---|---|---|---|---|---|---|---|
| Lose Power | Impatience | Not Listen | Stress | Conflict | Stress | Negative | Listen |
| Lose Position | Angry/Depressed | Control Others | Conflict | Conflict | Conflict | Negative | Ask Quest's |
| Divorce | Angry/Depressed | Denial/Mood Swings | Withdraw | Distant | Conflict | Hi Negative | Rebuild Reltns. |
| Health | Depressed | Binge +/- | Withdraw | Less Eff | Denial | Negative | Courage |
| Conflict | Avoid | Cowardice | Distrust | Errors | Conflict | Negative | Courage |
| Anxieties | | | | | | | |
| Promotion | Dominate | Over Talk | Resentment | Splitting | Lower Values | Negative | Team up |
| Be in Control | Posing | Not Real | Not Real | Distrust | Lower Values | Negative | Share |
| Parenting | Inconsistent | Binge +/- | Inconsistent | Anxiety | Lower Values | Negative | Do Right |
| Concerns | | | | | | | |
| Exercise/Diet | Denial | Unhealth | Schisms on Prsnl Habits | Schisms | Poor Modeling | Hi Negative | Exercise/Diet |
| Finances | Worry | Greed | Distracted | Anxiety | Lower Values | Negative | Support Others |
| Sleep/Rest | Fatigue | Low Hardiness | Unfocused | Errors | Poor Modeling | Hi Negative | Sleep/Rest |
| Friends | Favoritism | Favoritism | Favorites | Splitting | Poor Modeling | Negative | Honor All |
| Competence | Take Credit | Egotism | Distrust | Conflict | Poor Modeling | Negative | Admit/Change |

## Figure 15.3.  My Old Behaviors, New Behaviors, and Accountabilities

| Old Behaviors | New Behaviors | Accountabilities |
|---|---|---|
|  |  |  |
|  |  |  |
|  |  |  |
|  |  |  |

## Figure 15.4.  Sample Chart of Old Behaviors, New Behaviors, and Accountabilities

| Old Behaviors | New Behaviors | Accountabilities |
|---|---|---|
| Give orders | Listen effectively | Weekly feedback from A, B, C |
| Impatience | Ask more questions | Weekly feedback from A, J, K |
| Anger | Count to 10: no yelling | Weekly feedback from R, S |
| Play favorites | Encourage everyone | Monthly feedback from A, T, X |

*People:*
   ABC: Direct reports
   JKR: Peers
   RST: Superiors
      X: Boss

# 16

# THE COURAGE TO CHANGE

One man with courage makes a majority.

—*Andrew Jackson*

Rick Yenovkian was a highly principled, slapstick-funny, joyously relational, and intellectually gifted law student. He was the favorite son of the Sacramento County District Attorney's Office where he interned, the person everyone wanted for a dinner partner, and an exceptional four-sport letterman. Perhaps all were drawn to him merely because he was trustworthy, loyal, helpful, friendly, courteous, kind, obedient, cheerful, thrifty, brave, clean, and reverent.

One summer day in 1976, Rick awoke to find himself attached to machines and monitors. He could see that someone was holding his hand, but he was strangely numb.

"He's awake," said a voice. Rick could say nothing. He was told that while diving, he had struck a hidden underwater concrete pier, injuring his spinal cord and leaving him with catastrophic quadriplegia. This charismatic, caring, robustly powerful man now had but the thinnest influence over a few of his muscles from the neck up.

He was on a breathing machine.

"You're going to have to learn how to breathe," said a nurse. "You've lost the autonomic function." She smiled. "We'll show you how."

Rick relearned breathing and mastered the wheelchair. He studied and passed California's famously difficult bar exam and was sworn in as a deputy district attorney, where he has served with incomparable competence and zeal since 1977. When I joined the office after release from the Army, Rick helped orient me to the shop, to the courts, and to the civilian practice of law. His positive heart, camaraderie, good cheer, optimism, discipline, integrity, and guts inspire and uplift everyone in the court system. I believe that hardened criminals have been positively influenced by being so decently prosecuted by Rick.

In 2000, the California District Attorneys' Association recognized Rick Yenovkian as the state's Prosecutor of the Year, an award he merits every day. It saw what those who know, trust, love, and depend on him have always known: his character map has an unmatched integrity, a commitment to the rule of law, a fierce advocacy for victims, and an unflagging courage for principle.

Every day, Rick prepares for work the way NASA astronauts prepare for a moon shot. Everyday, Rick works under a different gravity.

Rick hasn't met Susan Beller yet, but he'd like her. Sue was a top Chicago tax attorney in love with Joe, her CPA husband. They enjoyed the life of newlywed professionals without children, frequenting the theater and museums and boating on the lake. Life was idyllic until Joe's recurring headaches revealed the presence of an inoperable brain tumor. Only one program on the planet offered the remote possibility of an experimental cure. Sue instantly sold their home, left her practice, and without family, friends, or job, moved Joe to the UC San Francisco Medical Center. There he underwent risky radiation treatments that left him sterile.

I was at a California State Bar conference when a person bursting with good cheer stopped me. I brilliantly sensed (1) that life must be very easy for her and (2) that I knew her. I was wrong on both counts.

"My name is Sue Beller," she said. "I can write professional educational material. Here's a sample I created for an upcoming tax seminar. Please forgive my boldness, but I want to work for you and I need a job. My husband is a patient at UCSF; you'd be buying my education products but not my presence. I'll take whatever pay you decide is right." She proved far worthier than the compensation.

Sue then learned that Joe's sterility had been exaggerated, for she was pregnant. On a quiet autumn day, after a valiant struggle in which Sue's courage rose rather than flagged, Joe passed away.

Sue's wonderful son, Joey, arrived in 1994. He is a strikingly handsome and dear young man, but this child of gifted parents, loved so unconditionally by his attentive mother, was probably affected by the heavy experimental radiation. He has never uttered a word.

Throughout, Sue sacrificed her promising legal career to remain in the constant company of her husband and now her son. She remains cheerful, upbeat, and positive, working for faith organizations that provide her the flexibility to care for Joey and to take him to experimental programs that hold the promise of enhancing his quality of relating to others.

She knew it would be wrong to give fear and negative feelings dominion over her life and her precious relationships.

Courage is facing fear rather than denying it; it is rushing forward to face the problem, to confront the giant whose shadow looms larger in our imagination than in reality.

It is fiercely exercising the daily disciplines of courageous behavior and consciously rejecting the gradual immersion into cycles of poor behaviors, stress-driven decisions, and anxious relationships.

Even better, you can grow your courage to become a person of strength and character without waiting for a dramatic and life-changing incident. Every day we receive new opportunities to demonstrate courage for others.

This begins with the courage to change behaviors. It ends with our commitment to accountability for those changes.

It is that simple. If this sounds daunting, we should ask, *why?* For we are fortunate; our opportunities to develop courage are in this very place.

In America, we are invited to build not only fine minds and robust careers but also, more crucially, our courage, our passport to living rightly. We may not like it, but of those who have much, much is expected.

When we strive to build our character first, we obey teachings so ancient and enduringly truthful that they reach back to Moses, Aristotle, and Confucius.

Presume for a moment that the ancient philosophers—the lovers of knowledge and the folks we had to study in college—are more accurate in their assessments of human nature than today's media advertisers.

With that presumption, you can set your sail against the popular culture. This is not a bad thing, for our culture pitches economic unease, political paranoia, work dread, life stress, health fears, ethical gridlock, moral obesity, mass divorces, hordes of angry ignored teens, persistent hesitancy, and chronic timidity. Perhaps I have understated it.

We remain in a common boat on a shared voyage in which the sum of our behaviors defines our community and our quality of courage.

As your coach, I ask you to look into the eyes of your colleagues, into the souls of your children, and into the moral responsibilities of our unique freedoms. You will see looking back at you a common need for courageous words, courageous leadership, and bold and principled modeling.

That is the path. On that path, you can fulfill the promise of your unique life and the special lives of those with whom you work and live.

You can stretch, use, and robustly strengthen the muscles of your character and of your newly awakened courage. With courage, you can open doors for your organization, for your family, and for your life.

You can be the singer of the hymn, the chorus for Garth Brooks, and model for others the words he wrote in the song "Belleau Wood": *Heaven's not beyond the clouds, it's just beyond the fear.*[1]

I've told you stories of people who, like you, faced crises that tested their guts and who, in brave response, lived songs of strength and courage. They felt fear at their Points of Decision. But first, they stood fast. They dug down to intentionally embrace the courage that has been installed in every person. They boldly used that courage to align their behaviors with their high core values. They did this for others, for their organizations, and for their families.

You are no different from them. Kay, Thieneman, Whitwam, Stein, Schwarzkopf, Murray, Tu, Bodenheimer, Baring, Shaw, Long, Yu, Beller, and Yenovkian have all faced fear and been the better for it. Within the bindings of this book, they speak to you, offering comradeship.

I know what they would say to you: that it is not only possible for all of us to prevail against fear but that this is the only logical option.

They overcame their inborn resistance to conflict and by doing so inspired others to accomplishments beyond imagination.

We learn and teach courage by modeling. When we see or hear a story of courage, we can own the tale. Courage grows in community. The stories in this and other books are now yours.

We all stand in the ring of life.

Your coach, although seemingly distant, stands with you, seeing in you the eyes of possibility.

For regardless of position, we all lead and influence others with the stories of our lives and the values of our hearts. We affect each other. In this way, we are hopelessly related.

With this relatedness, we can dispirit others, or we can inspire.

What is your story as you approach your Point of Decision?

Like Coach Tony, I encourage you to go into the world with good courage, holding fast to all that is good, honoring all persons, facing our fears, and robustly living rightly and boldly.

It is our birthright to strive for principles and to relate to each other according to things greater than ourselves. This is our opportunity to practice, model, and embrace courage, the first of all human qualities.

# Notes

## Introduction

1. Tim Kasser uses available global empirical data to show us that people who strive for wealth tend to live with lower well-being regardless of age, income, or culture. Tim Kasser, *The High Price of Materialism* (Cambridge, Mass.: MIT Press, 2002).

## Chapter Two

1. Anne Lamott, *Operating Instructions: A Journal of My Son's First Year* (New York: Pantheon, 1993), p. 10.
2. Stephen L. Carter, *Integrity* (New York: HarperCollins, 1996), p. 46.
3. Jim Collins, *Good to Great: Why Some Companies Make the Leap . . . and Others Don't* (New York: HarperCollins, 2001), pp. 17–22.
4. Ibid., p. 194.
5. Ibid., pp. 1, 16.
6. Ronnie Lott (USC), Eric Wright (Missouri), Carlton Williamson (Pittsburgh), Fred Dean (San Diego Chargers), Jack "Hacksaw" Reynolds (Los Angeles Rams), and Dwight Hicks (Philadelphia health food store). All became All-Pro's; Lott, Montana, and Walsh are in the NFL Hall of Fame; Dean is a nominee. The 49ers are one of two teams to win five Super Bowls and the only professional team that is 5–0 in world championships.

## Chapter Three

1. The first two parts are from Carter, *Integrity*, p. 7; the third is my own. Carter's third part is "Saying openly that you are acting on your understanding of right and wrong." I thank Professor Carter for his Mosaic and Aristotelian accomplishments.
2. This works for everyone except sociopaths.
3. Charlie Murray, West Point Class of 1962, a legendary leader in combat and in law, is cited as an example in the Army leadership training manual. Serving in Vietnam as a rifle company commander, Charlie was directed by his battalion commander to relieve one of his platoon leaders for an incident that had embarrassed the battalion commander. Charlie said, "Sir, my platoon leader did everything I asked him to do. I find no fault in his performance. If you want to relieve someone, you'd better relieve me." The battalion commander rescinded the order.

## Chapter Four

1. Ted Barris, *Days of Victory* (Markham, Ontario, Canada: Allen & Son, 2005).

## Chapter Six

1. M. Wensing, H. P. Jung, J. Mainz, F. Olesen, and R. Grol, "A Systematic Review of the Literature on Patient Priorities for General Practice Care. Part 1: Description of the Research Domain," *Social Science Medicine*, 1998, *47*, 1573–1588.
2. To protect privacy, the names of the physician-participants have been changed; the planners and trainers—Terry Stein, Bob Tull, and Robbie Pearl—appear under their true names.
3. Insurance reports to the State Bar committee on liability insurance, professional responsibility, and the division of legal competence, 1980–1991.

4. James Patterson and Peter Kim, *The Day America Told the Truth* (Upper Saddle River, N.J.: Prentice Hall), 1991, pp. 142–143. Patterson and Kim, executives with the J. Walter Thompson advertising agency, discovered in the largest survey of American morals that popular respect plummeted for the ethics of most professions. Lawyers were ranked 56th out of 71 professions, below bartenders, cab drivers, prison guards, and soap opera actors.

5. State Bar of California Survey of the Membership, Office of Legal Education and Competence, 1991; chief investigator, Karen Betzner, J.D.; various reports from the Office of Legal Education to the Board of Governors, State Bar of California, 1989–1992.

6. Douglas McGregor, *The Human Side of Enterprise* (New York: McGraw-Hill, 1960).

7. Chris Argyris, "Immaturity-Maturity Theory," Accel Team, 2004 [http://accel-team.com/human_relations/hrels_06ii_argyris.html].

8. Food and Drug Administration, *Supervisory Leadership. Module 2: Effective Communication* (Rockville, Md.: Food and Drug Administration, n.d.).

9. Joe Flower, "Human Change by Design: Excerpts from a Conversation with Robert R. Blake, Ph.D.," *Healthcare Forum Journal*, 1992, *35*, 84–89.

10. Collins, *Good to Great*; James C. Collins and Jerry I. Porras, *Built to Last: Successful Habits of Visionary Companies* (New York: HarperCollins, 1994); Bill Catlette and Richard Hadden, *Contented Cows Give Better Milk: The Plain Truth About Employee Relations and Your Bottom Line* (Germantown, Tenn.: Saltillo Press, 2001); Robert Levering, *A Great Place to Work: What Makes Some Employers So Good (and Most So Bad)* (San Francisco: Great Place to Work Institute, 1988).

11. Collins, *Good to Great*, pp. 3 and 7. Since Collins's book was published, it came to light that one firm, Fannie Mae, fabricated its profits. The Securities and Exchange Commission did not

agree with Fannie Mae and indicated that Fannie Mae might be
required to justify previously unreported losses of some $9 bil-
lion (*Corporate Reform Weekly*, Dec. 20, 2004). When that firm
is included in the original profitability study, the eleven aver-
aged 6.88 times the market. Without Fannie Mae, the average
becomes 6.817, which is not a material difference. In addition
to Fannie Mae, the *Good to Great* companies were Abbott, Cir-
cuit City, Gillette, Kimberly-Clark, Kroger, Nucor, Philip Morris,
Pitney Bowes, Walgreen's, and Wells Fargo.

## Chapter Seven

1. This is a variation on the medical or nursing instructional model
   "See one, Do one, Teach one" and is further reflected in the Inte-
   grenómics motto, "Learn, Do, Be."
2. Dr. Smith is a composite of three TPMG physicians.
3. Theodore Lipps, "Empathy, Inner Imitation, and Sense Feelings" (1903), trans. Melvin Rader and Max Schertel, in Melvin
   Rader, *A Modern Book of Aesthetics*, 5th ed. (Austin, Tex.: Holt,
   Rinehart and Winston, 1979), pp. 371–378.

## Chapter Eight

1. Dale Carnegie, *How to Win Friends and Influence People* (New
   York: Pocket Books, 1990), p. 14. Originally published in 1937.
2. Action-e-Reactions are similar to "'I' statements," which appear
   in psychology, education, communication, and child psychology
   works (for example, see http://www.colorado.edu/conflict/peace/
   treatment/istate.htm). Action-e-Reactions are also similar to
   the SBI (situation, behavior, and impact) statements developed
   so successfully by the Center for Creative Leadership.
3. James M. Kouzes and Barry Z. Posner, *Encouraging the Heart: A
   Leader's Guide to Rewarding and Recognizing Others* (San Francisco: Jossey-Bass, 1999).
4. Kenneth Blanchard and Spencer Johnson, *The One Minute
   Manager* (New York: Morrow, 1982), p. 40.

## Chapter Ten

1. Peter F. Drucker, in "Quotes," *The Performance Edge*, 2004, 1 [http://www.kelcon.com/E-News.First%20Edition.htm].
2. Warren Bennis and Burt Nanus, *Leaders: Strategies for Taking Charge*, 2nd ed. (New York: HarperCollins, 2003), pp. ix, 20.
3. Steven Covey, *The 7 Habits of Highly Effective People: Powerful Lessons in Personal Change* (New York: Simon & Schuster, 1989), p. 101.
4. Max De Pree, M. (1989). *Leadership Is an Art* (New York: Dell, 1989), p. 131.
5. Peter F. Drucker, "Foreword," in Frances Hesselbein, Marshall Goldsmith, and Richard Beckhard (eds.), *The Leader of the Future: New Visions, Strategies, and Practices for the Next Era.* (San Francisco: Jossey-Bass, 1996), p. xii.
6. Lao Tzu, quoted in Gordon S. Jackson, *Never Scratch a Tiger with a Short Stick* (Colorado Springs: NavPress, 2003), p. 105.
7. H. Norman Schwarzkopf, quoted in Dana Durbin, "Schwarzkopf Shares Insights," Rice University Office of News and Media Relations, Sept. 24, 1998 [http://www.media.rice.edu/media/NewsBot.asp?MODE=VIEW&ID=4332&SnID=70249175].
8. Sun Tzu, quoted in James Clavell, *The Art of War* (New York: Dell, 1983), p. 2.
9. Used in University of Maryland business classes I taught and in others.
10. Personal communication with Dean Currie, former associate dean for administration and policy planning at Harvard University's Graduate School of Business Administration, 1996.
11. Casey A. Neff (ed.), *Bugle Notes*, 95th ed (West Point, N.Y.: United States Military Academy, 2003), p. 4.

## Chapter Eleven

1. All names have been changed except for John Gerdelman's. "Mike Keegan" represents the experience of three MCI directors.

"Payton Neelum" represents a number of C-level executives at that time.

2. Kouzes and Posner, *Encouraging the Heart*, p. 4.

## Chapter Fourteen

1. Deanna Caputo and David Dunning, "What You Don't Know: The Role Played by Errors of Omission in Imperfect Self-Assessments," *Journal of Experimental Social Psychology*, 2005, *41*, 488–505.

## Chapter Fifteen

1. Jim Collins, *Good to Great* (New York: HarperCollins, 2001), pp. 13, 41.

2. Robert J. House (ed.), *Culture, Leadership, and Organizations* (Sage, 2004). House, of the Wharton School of Management, University of Pennsylvania, conceived of a global study to learn if leadership characteristics are universally endorsed. The resulting Global Leadership and Organizational Behavior Effectiveness (GLOBE) Project conducted an extended 1990s study of more than seventeen thousand managers in 62 nations and 951 organizations. It learned that there is a global perception of organizational and leadership rights and wrongs. The top GLOBE-endorsed leader traits:

> *Negative:* asocial, irritable, dictatorial, ruthless, egocentric, uncooperative, a loner
>
> *Positive:* trustworthy, encouraging, communicative, just, honest, dependable, cooperative, a team player

## Chapter Sixteen

1. John Henry and Garth Brooks, "Belleau Wood," copyright © 1997 Cool Hand Music/Major Bob Music/No Fences Music (ASCAP).

# Acknowledgments

Our love to our children Jena and Eric, whose courageous commitment to service inspires all. To Danny and Jessica, for their courage to persist, to try, and to persevere.

Our thanks to the courageous people whose stories compose this book. The roots of the writing connect to others with courage: Mary Tzu, Ying Lee, Elinor and John Hause, Lars Stenberg, Max Kelley, Sara Ying Rounsaville, Anna Lagìos, Eva Chrysanthe, and their families; parents Da-tsien Tzu, Tsung-chi Lee, Robert and Maralyn Elliott; "Miss" Nina Molleson; and our Shanghai family, Li Huo-sun, Li Chin, Li Lulu, and their families; Toussaint Streat, Coach Tony, Pinoy Punsalong, Don Stewart, Sally Craft, and the YMCA staff; Fire Battalion Chief Jack Peeff, General H. Norman Schwarzkopf, Sergeant Major George Kihara, Ruby Dyer, Professors K. C. Liu, Edgar Bodenheimer, Jim Edwards, and John Riker, Charles A. Murray, Robin Shakely, John Goldthorpe, Scott Prentice, Rick Yenovkian and Steve Masuda, Diane Richardson, the Gang, and the Sacramento County Office of the District Attorney; FBI Special Agent Charles Hickey, Herbert Rosenthal, Diane C. Yu, Mark Harris, Terry Stein, Bob Tull, John Prosser, Professor Mary Ellen Jones, Sally Folsom, Louis De Mattei, author Annie Lamott, and my teachers, coaches, booksellers, and librarians.

To my colleagues at the Center for Creative Leadership, OPM, WMDC, and the U.S. Department of Justice and to Dave Jones, James Sullivan, Len Marrella, Ed Ruggero, Bill Cater, Steve Wilson, Gary Steele, Toby Quirk, Tammy Toso, Don McCabe, Pat Toffler, John Truslow, Jeff Weart, LTC Bill Stringer, Hon. Eugene Sullivan,

General Fred Franks Jr., and the other brothers and sisters of West Point's National Conference on Ethics in America. To David Kai Tu, Eric Becker, John Smiley, Rob Daugherty, Barry Shiller, Frank Ramirez, Paul Watermulder, Paul Benchener, Chuck Pappalardo, Bob Laird, Ike Elliott, Tom Baker, Steve Schibsted, and the Top Gun men, who hold me accountable and keep the flame bright. To the Blood: Water Mission, 1000 Wells Project, and Jars of Clay. A son and brother's gratitude, as always, to West Point and the USMA Class of 1968 and Company A-3, for teaching and modeling moral and physical courage.

Warm thanks to our fine editors and colleagues at Jossey-Bass: Susan Williams, Byron Schneider, Mary Garrett, Bruce Emmer, Carolyn Carlstroem, Matt Kaye, Kasi Miller, Rob Brandt, and the rest of the crew for their expertise, tireless wisdom and guidance, and attention to detail.

We can never sufficiently thank our agents, Jane Dystel and Miriam Goderich of the Dystel-Goderich Literary Agency, and my "sister" Amy Tan, who together have made our writing career possible and facilitated our commitment to be full-time parents.

# The Authors

GUS LEE is an ethicist, author, leadership consultant, executive coach, and former corporate VP, senior executive, senior deputy district attorney, Army JAG, ethics whistleblower, paratrooper, and legal counsel for U.S. Senate ethics investigations. He managed California's legal education for its 140,000 attorneys and was the lead trainer for the state's prosecutors. He grew up in an African American ghetto, was raised by YMCA boxers and mentored by H. Norman Schwarzkopf at West Point, by Nuremberg prosecutor and Holocaust refugee Edgar Bodenheimer and Yenching scholar K. C. Liu at UC Davis. He has taught leadership at Bank of America, Centura, DEA, ISEC, FBI, Kaiser Permanente, Levi Strauss, the U.S. Department of Justice, West Point, Whirlpool, law firms and nonprofit institutions; has worked with executives from Caterpillar Mexico, Franklin Investments, Homeland Defense, Kodak, Nestlé, NASA, NORAD, Pfizer, Johnson & Johnson, Stora Enso, and Xerox; and is an adjunct for the Center for Creative Leadership, the Office of Personnel Management, and the U.S. Department of Justice.

He has written five best-sellers; optioned two for film; written for *Time* and the *Encyclopaedia Britannica*; addressed the National Conference of Supreme Court Justices, Smithsonian Institution, Young Presidents, many colleges, and many national organizations; performed more than two hundred criminal jury trials; won many military and civilian awards; and spoken on *CBS This Morning*, CNN, NPR, and Voice of America. Happily married since 1979, he

and Diane have highly principled young adult children and are raising Danny, a wonderful teen from an immigrant family, while walking Pooki the Wonder Dog.

DIANE ELLIOTT-LEE received her M.S.N. cum laude in psychiatric
nursing from the University of Nebraska, Omaha, and her B.S.N.
with high distinction from the University of Northern Colorado. She
has been a multiple award-winning clinical nurse specialist, hospital-
wide ethics committee member, and medical school clinical faculty
at the University of California San Francisco and UC Davis medical
centers. She has served as adjunct faculty for Beth-El College of Nursing at the University of Colorado at Colorado Springs and as a leadership consultant to hospitals and health care organizations.

Given the choice between pursuing her dynamic career and
raising her children, she made the courageous decision to leave the
first to focus on the second. She has been active in youth, community, and church activities while volunteering for the American
Red Cross and advocating for principled nursing education, the
care of untended teens, and rational student life.

Diane has helped edit Gus's five previous books and provided
guidance, inspiration, and structure for this one.

# Index